Devotional Companion
to the
International Lessons

Abingdon Press
Nashville

DEVOTIONAL COMPANION TO THE INTERNATIONAL LESSONS

Copyright © 1994 by Abingdon Press

All rights reserved.
No part of this work may be reproduced or transmitted in any form or by any means, electronic or mechanical, including photocopying and recording, or by any information storage or retrieval system, except as may be expressly permitted by the 1976 Copyuright Act or in writing from the publisher. Requests for permission should be addressed in writing to Abingdon Press, 201 Eighth Avenue South, Nashville, TN 37203.

This book is printed on recycled, acid-free paper.

ISBN 0-687-08635-3
ISSN 1074-9918

Scripture quotations are from the New Revised Standard Version Bible, Copyright 1989 by the Division of Christian Education of the National Council of the Churches of Christ in the USA. Used by permission.

94 95 96 97 98 99 00 01 02 03 – 10 9 8 7 6 5 4 3 2 1

MANUFACTURED IN THE UNITED STATES OF AMERICA

Hymnals Referenced

B   Forbis, Wesley, ed. *The Baptist Hymnal.* Nashville: Covention Press, 1991.

C   *The Cokesbury Worship Hymnal.* Nashville: Abingdon Press, 1966.

E   Glover, Raymond, ed. *The Hymnal 1982.* New York: The Church Hymnal Corporation, 1985.

F   Bock, Fred, ed. *Hymns for the Family of God.* Nashville: Paragon Associates, Inc., 1976.

L   *Lutheran Book of Worship.* Minneapolis: Augsburg Publishing House, 1978.

P   McKim, LindaJo, ed. *The Presbyterian Hymnal.* Louisville: Westminster/John Knox Press, 1990.

UM   Young, Carlton R., ed. *The United Methodist Hymnal.* Nashville: The United Methodist Publishing House, 1989.

W   Batastini, Robert J., ed. *Worship.* Chicago: GIA Publications, Inc., 1986.

Preface

Most persons who use the devotions in this book are doing so because they are involved in a study of God's Word through the International Lesson Series. No matter which of the denominational or nondenominational Bible study materials used, this devotional guide is appropriate for the class that wants to have a time of worship to open its study. We invite you to spend a few minutes with these materials if you are the class leader. Use them to gently move you from the modern world to the Bible world and back again. In the classroom setting, you should read the Scripture and either read the devotional or retell it in your own words.

These devotions give you a complete worship resource. They begin with the Scriptures prescribed by the Uniform Lesson Series. These Scriptures are carefully chosen to relate to the Scripture lessons used in your curriculum. We have added a Psalm and two hymn suggestions, all of which relate to the Scripture passage in a meaningful way. The hymns suggested are found in eight denominational hymnals and the most popular nondenominational hymnals.

The devotions themselves are carefully prepared from the same outlines as the International Lessons. You should easily be able to find the parallels. They are structured in two parts. The first is a short study of the Scripture text. It explains something of the historical, biblical context, some textual background, and what the Scripture says. The second part moves the newfound scriptural knowledge into a twentieth-century

DEVOTIONAL COMPANION TO THE INTERNATIONAL LESSONS

context. It seeks to answer for each participant the question What does this Scripture mean to me today?

While this book is designed to accompany the International Lessons, the material will easily stand alone for a personal time of mediation and worship.

With Scripture reading, singing (if you like), Bible study, and contemporary and personal devotions, this *Devotional Companion to the International Lessons* gives you a complete program in ten minutes. May you find each devotional a rewarding experience.

September 4, 1994

READ IN YOUR BIBLE: Joshua 1:1-9
SUGGESTED PSALM: 110
SUGGESTED HYMNS: Zion, Haste (B, C, E, F, L, UM)
   O God, Our Help in Ages Past (All)

Preparing for Victory

Joshua 1:1-9 is the beginning of an exciting phase of Israel's history. After their Egyptian captivity and forty years of wilderness wandering, the Hebrews now are permitted to enter into the land of promise. Moses has died, and the new generation of leadership is on the horizon.

Our text begins with the chronology of Israel's history after the death of Moses. Joshua, Moses' assistant, is charged by Yahweh to proceed to the promised land. The land represents the fulfillment of the promise of God to Israel, which goes all the way back to Yahweh's words to Abram: "Go from your country and your kindred and your father's house to the land that I will show you" (Genesis 12:1).

Yahweh also gives Joshua encouragement by saying the enemies of Israel will not be able to stand against them all the days of their lives. The Lord would also always be with them. This is only a slight variation in wording of Yahweh's original threefold promise to the matriarchs and patriarchs: land, descendants, and relationship with Yahweh.

As we read the history of Israel, even to this day, we see the strength of the promises of Yahweh. A small band of wanderers, with the Lord's help, become a great people from which the Messiah will come and, for Christians, has come.

* * *

Many adults will give of themselves for a cause to which they are deeply committed. Parents, for instance, sacrifice time and effort to coach their child's sports teams. This sacrifice, however, is not always given to more open-ended pursuits, for example, involvement in church or in a child's formal education. We often wonder why well-meaning parents neglect children's moral, spiritual, and intellectual development, yet are so involved in other facets of their lives.

A page from Israel's history illustrates this phenomenon. The more focused a community is on mission, the more dedicated its actions become. In moments of crisis—for example, the Exodus—Israel flees as a people with a mission of survival. Many adults seek protection and security for themselves and their families. In today's lesson, Israel is pulled back together by the charge to take possession of the land promised by Yahweh.

A crisis focuses people. While in the wilderness for forty years, Israel turns to self-made idols. Later, in a settled land, comes the temptation—as always—to turn to foreign gods and idols. When Israel is pressured and has a common purpose it remains steadfast. Troubles come when Israel loses focus and drifts from the center of God's purpose.

A church building program provides a modern example. As the church's program needs increase, or more worship space becomes necessary, a congregation plans facilities expansion. The church becomes more active, and people are drawn into the new mission. This is a time when most adults willingly cooperate. New members may be attracted. Why? Because the church has a common, focused purpose.

Often after a building program, an interlude occurs in a church's outreach. The community loses an immediate goal and rests from its great expenditure of energy. Like parents who can devote a short ball season to their children's lives but often fail to prepare for lifetime needs, a church excels when focusing on one short-term task.

When Israel is well-settled, religious devotion begins to wane. When survival is not a daily issue, other matters attract the people's attention. When modern people are in the midst of crisis (job or love loss, grave illness or death), then they, too, are more likely to call on the Lord. When calm is in the land or in the home, it is easy to misdirect gratitude.

For all of us, it is vital to realize that the gift of land is for Israel to share its God-relationship with others. This is the sharing task of the church as well. Everything we do, we do to share Christ's gospel with a world in need of good news.

Let us pray:
O God, help us hold fast to our vision of you and the promise you give to us through the holy Scripture. Focus our lives in your love for all people. In Christ's name, amen.

September 11, 1994
READ IN YOUR BIBLE: Hebrews 11:23-24
SUGGESTED PSALM: Psalm 131
SUGGESTED HYMNS: Faith of Our Fathers (B, C, F, L, UM, W)
    How Firm a Foundation (all)

Acting on Faith

Today's devotional lesson concerns faith as the driving force behind people's actions, both of individuals and of the nation of Israel. Joshua crosses the Jordan River with the people of Israel, going into the land of promise. Joshua 3 explicitly explains Yahweh's careful directions regarding the carrying of the Ark of the Covenant—a sign of God's presence with the people.

The accompanying devotional lesson, Hebrews 11:23-24, speaks about faith, related from the story of Moses—the prominent figure in Israel's Exodus. Moses was also the prophet who led Israel out of Egypt and through the wilderness for forty years. As the people prepare to inhabit the promised land, it is fitting for us to be reminded of Moses' heroic faith.

Chapter 11 in Hebrews has been called "the faith chapter" because verses 2-40 expand on the first: "Now faith is the assurance of things hoped for, the conviction of things not seen." A sort of "honor roll" of the faithful constitutes this chapter. In verse 23 Moses' parents are lifted up, both for their faith in hiding Moses and for their faith in being unafraid of the pharaoh's edict to kill all Hebrew males less than two years old.

Moses' faith is praised likewise, in verse 24, for giving Moses the courage to refuse identification with Pharaoh's household and choosing, rather, to be a child of Yahweh. It is by faith that God's people do the right things, which may put them at risk. The people of God, however, trust the Lord.

* * *

I have a friend who taught me discipleship's meaning in a very concrete way. My friend, whom I will call Jim, was a former member of one of the churches I served. Jim served in our small, struggling church in many ways.

Jim was president of a bank in a time when banks began to have economic difficulty. After he had been working there for about a year, its board of directors felt the bank needed to discipline some of its delinquent accounts. This was not unusual in those days, but the policy was put in force so quickly that many of the borrowers were caught short. However, bank policy is bank policy, and the board chose to foreclose on many accounts. People lost their homes and businesses.

Jim made a bold decision. Although he had a family and a good job, he told the bank directors that if they did not delay their policy implementation, he would resign. The bank did not, and Jim resigned. Without a new job prospect, he nonetheless let his conscience be his guide. He made me appreciate, in a new way, Christian commitment. "I could no longer work for people who put the bottom line ahead of the needs of people," he said.

Joshua and the people of Israel needed the assurance of things hoped for—faith in Yahweh—to go over into the land of promise. Joshua had already sent men to spy in Jericho, and they had been graciously received by Rahab, also one of those persons who is recounted in Hebrew's honor roll. This invasion of the promised land was a brazen step contemplated by Israel, but it was done in "the conviction of things not seen," by the people of God and their leader Joshua's deep faith in Yahweh.

Moses, too, had given up much because of the faith that made him one of Israel's most eminent leaders. Moses could have lived his life out in the ease of Pharaoh's house, but chose instead to be the human vehicle through which God's liberating power functioned "to let God's people go."

Even today, living among us are people whose faith is so authentic and trustworthy that they act on faith's conviction, knowing that the Lord will provide for their every need. Many adults seek assurance of safety when they face uncertainty and danger. All of us live in a difficult era. In our day, people need the words and actions of faith, assuring them of God's continuing presence. May we pray to be those who lead in the spirit of "the conviction of things not seen."

Let us pray:
Gracious and faithful Lord, into your hands we commit our lives. Place in us the courage to stand faith's ground and remember the sacrifice Jesus made on our behalf. Ground us in the faith that makes true disciples. Amen.

September 18, 1994

READ IN YOUR BIBLE: Psalm 149
SUGGESTED PSALM: Same
SUGGESTED HYMNS: When in Our Music God Is Glorified (B, E, L, P, UM, W)
Come, We That Love the Lord (B, C, E, F, UM, W)

Obeying God

This psalm begins and ends with a call to joyful worship. The opening and closing phrases consist of the same jubilant expression: "Praise the Lord," or "Hallelujah."

We are struck, as we read the first five verses, by the enthusiasm of Israel's song. The people are directed to sing, praise, dance, rejoice, and make melody with the tambourine and the lyre. Israel's purpose in vigorous celebration is to remember Yahweh as Sovereign, with thanksgiving as the celebration's keynote. Yahweh has given humble Israel victory over "the nations," salvation from Israel's enemies.

Those who read this psalm carefully are struck by the transition, however, in verse 6. What follows on the emotive character of Israel's public worship is a call to action: a two-edged sword in their hands, executing vengeance on the nations, punishment on the peoples.

If this psalm is an indicator of the nature of Israel's worship, then Israel threw its whole being into worship and praise of God. If we can remember that for much of its history Israel was an oppressed people, then we can understand their vigor in worshiping a God who will give them vengeance over their enemies.

* * *

I have heard it said that people want to support a winner. I think this is true. When we think of the enthusiasm and money spent on professional sports, we marvel that whole cities catch the enthusiasm of winning teams. These are cities that cannot agree on teachers' salaries or housing for the poor. These cities often have acrimonious city council meetings. Yet, let one of their sports teams be in the World Series or the Super Bowl, however, and it becomes a city of "brotherly love"!

Most people want to be a part of a successful venture. This

was no less true in ancient Israel. Yahweh is often depicted as a warrior God in Hebrew Scriptures. Yahweh showed favor to Israel, according to their belief, by granting victory against their enemies, and if Yahweh withheld favor from Israel, they were defeated. This same attitude can be seen in people today. When misfortune befalls them, they may ask, "What did I do to deserve this?"

One truth in Scripture is the repeated theme: When people are obedient to God, they prosper. There may be an exception here and there—Job's story, for instance—but generally, when people follow the word of God, they prosper. Our lesson this morning from Joshua is a case in point. The Lord gives very explicit instructions for capturing the city of Jericho. The people of Israel follow these instructions and take the city of Jericho. No mystery involved.

In a way, we could say that we are given explicit instructions about how to be on God's winning side, as it were. The psalmist writes of the worship life of those who love God. Worshiping people praise the Lord though dance, song, and making melody with the tambourine and the lyre. This is the command of the Lord. Note that the psalmist does not urge the people to worship only if it is convenient, but rather assumes that people who love God will worship God.

When people really want to connect with God and each other, they risk looking foolish by singing and dancing and praising God. They do this together because in their shared enthusiasm is their unity. Perhaps to others their worship looks foolish, but to God it looks wise. Paul said it best: "But God chose what is foolish in the world to shame the wise; God chose what is weak in the world to shame the strong" (1 Corinthians 1:27).

Let us pray:

O God, help us to regain the fervor we first had when we turned our hearts toward you. Fill us with the spirit of enthusiasm about the plan you have for our lives and for the life of your church. It is our worship that connects us as brothers and sisters. Create anew our hearts in praise. Amen.

September 25, 1994

READ IN YOUR BIBLE: Psalm 116:12-19
SUGGESTED PSALM: Psalm 116
SUGGESTED HYMNS: O Worship the King (B, C, E, F, L, P, UM)
There Is a Balm in Gilead (B, E, F, P, UM, W)

Making Choices

Our reading begins with the question "What shall I return to the LORD for all his bounty to me?" (Psalm 116:12). The balance of the psalm relates the psalmist's vows to the Lord for answering prayers for healing, which are spoken in the first verses of this psalm.

The psalmist answers his own question as we read the phrase "I will" four different times. I will: lift up the cup of salvation, pay my vows (twice), offer to you a thanksgiving sacrifice. As is usually the case, the Lord's action comes first and is followed by the devoted person's vow of faithfulness. The human response to God is the human side of covenant making.

Note where these vows of faithfulness occur. They are not offered in the secrecy of a prayer closet (see Matthew 6:6). Rather, the psalmist makes the vows twice "in the presence of all the LORD's people." Thus the sacred oaths offered are part of a public confession offered in public worship.

* * *

I heard a preacher once say that the reason why many people are secretive about their financial dealings with the church is because possessions are usually the last idol many of us are willing to relinquish. She said people were secretive because they were ashamed of what they gave. Is it true that many of us are very quiet about the things over which we feel shame?

This comes to mind after reading Psalm 116:12-19. The psalmist's intentions are so vocal and loud it is almost startling. There is little doubt about the psalmist's future course of action—it is decisive, and it is public. Many adults hesitate to make long-term commitments, but not the singer of this psalm.

Bold indeed is the person who will publicly proclaim the intentions of his or her life. This public announcement also points to the sacredness of the gathered assembly. We see how indispensable the community of faith is for our individual lives. Could this be why, even today, we celebrate many of our own sacred vows in the sanctuary of our churches: marriage, baptisms, and memorial services for departed saints? It is difficult to keep vows. Perhaps, part of a community's gift to itself is to help each person remain on the path of his or her promises of God.

Most of us do not remember church meetings vividly. Most of them are usually matter of fact, though important. But I remember one church meeting that was different. The administrative board had been struggling for about ninety minutes with its annual budget. They had disputed, trying to cut a little here and a little there from the upcoming year's budget. In the room of about forty people a long-time member stood. She waited until everyone was quiet.

In a muted, but unyielding, voice she said, "Walter and I have seen this church give itself a budget year in and year out that forced its ministry to only limp along. Like everyone else, we thought someone else would make up the yearly shortfall. Since this has never happened, we have decided to tithe the next three years. It is time for us to live up to our church vows, instead of expecting Christ's church to live down to our noncommittal stewardship." The board was absolutely silent for some time, before they voted not to cut the budget.

After this well-respected woman's words to her church, it has never had financial difficulty since. Most adults make life-shaping commitments, but this decision was also church changing. For too long, most of the members had possessed an attitude that they would do as little as possible to get by.

Joshua knew whom he would serve, as did the psalmist writing for us today. One convicted layperson, along with her husband, made a public vow of faith, which allowed a church to be reborn. All of us can make this kind of decision. May we make it with conviction.

Let us pray:
Lord of our life and heart, help us this day to know you in our worship. As you have answered the prayers of our hearts, work through us to answer the prayers of others. Make us ever mindful that you work through us to do wonderful things for your people. In Christ's name we pray. Amen.

October 2, 1994

READ IN YOUR BIBLE: Psalm 81:6-16
SUGGESTED PSALM: Psalm 81
SUGGESTED HYMNS: Dear Lord and Father of Mankind (B, C, E, F, L, P, UM)
My Shepherd Will Supply My Need (B, E, F, P, W)

Choices Have Consequences

It is helpful to know that the first five verses of Psalm 81 speak in worship language about Yahweh's great claim on the chosen people. The psalm's balance reexamines Yahweh's actions for Israel and what Israel's God expects from them.

Verse 6's grace note is the last phrase of verse 5, which, in the NRSV, follows a blank space inserted in the text. This is done to show that a new thought is presented. In Israel's defining story—the Exodus—the Hebrews endured heavy forced labor by the Egyptians, hence the psalm's allusions to the "shoulder of burden" and the "hands freed."

In the story of the Exodus, the Lord hears the people's cry of affliction and brings them out of Egypt with a mighty hand and an outstretched arm. The "secret place of thunder" is Sinai, and the "wilderness place" where God tested the people is Meribah.

The psalm continues by urging the people to hear the Lord's word delivered by their present priest. They are to continue listening to the Lord, live in obedience to the Lord, and shun "strange gods." The former disobedience of Israel is recounted with the attached promises of the Lord's blessing to those who are now faithful to him. If faithfulness is Israel's choice, not only will Israel's enemies be subdued by Yahweh, but Israel will be sustained by the finest wheat and honey as well.

* * *

Mr. Bates, a very nice man, was my neighbor as I grew up. He always took time to play baseball with the neighborhood children, and I loved him because he taught me how to throw a curve ball. He took his family to church every Sunday morning and Wednesday night. He always gave to his church, and we all knew it was an important part of his life.

Mr. Bates died relatively young in life, but he left each of his five children enough money to attend college. This surprised many, since his job did not pay a great deal of money. His son told me that with every paycheck his father received, he gave 10 percent to his church and put 10 percent into a fund for his children's education. This plan was invariable. His family accepted living on 80 percent of his take-home pay.

Mr. Bates's life was a testimony that one's choices in life make a difference. Some adults switch loyalties easily. Mr. Bates was not one of these. Early in his life he decided that he desired his children to have educational opportunities that he never had. Thus for over twenty-five years, twice a month, Mr. Bates saved because he had made a decision and had a plan.

Today we live in a society where many folks think about the quick road to success, whether it be financial, professional, or spiritual. The truth is, in this life, good habits are forged over time by a word that many see as outmoded—*discipline.* If one wants to do something well, then a great deal of time must be set aside to practice it, for instance playing a musical instrument or learning a foreign language. As my father was fond of saying, "if something is worth doing, then it is worth doing well." To do something well is to love it—and we always spend time with the things we love!

It amazes me that people often say that they wish they knew the Bible, but they rarely take time to read and study it. Dick Murray, one of my seminary professors, has often said, "People want to want to study the Bible; they don't want to study the Bible." There is great wisdom in this.

Our psalm suggests that choices have consequences. Each day we make choices about what we eat or how we spend our time. If we love God, then it might help us to make choices that develop "holy habits" of prayer, Scripture study, and reflection on our lives in the arms of our loving God. People who love God choose daily to spend time with the Lord—a time when a relationship with God develops and God is with us.

Let us pray:
Almighty God, you have condescended to come near to us in Christ Jesus. Give us this day the will and courage to practice with our lives the conviction of our lips. Make us your people by the discipline of a life forged by holy habits. Amen.

October 9, 1994

READ IN YOUR BIBLE: Psalm 33:10-22
SUGGESTED PSALM: Psalm 33
SUGGESTED HYMNS: Open My Eyes That I May See (B, C, F, P, UM)
There's a Wideness in God's Mercy (all)

God Chooses and Empowers

This psalm is straightforward in its faith expression and shows the great faith of the psalmist by contrasting this faith with the faith of mortals in human plans. The contrast is best seen in the difference between the Lord's ways and the ways of the nations and the nations' kings and armies.

The psalmist sings that the Lord's words last forever, while the counsels of the nations are brought to nothing by the Lord. We even read a beatitude: "Happy is the nation whose God is the LORD" (33:12). This says, in effect, that if a nation follows Yahweh, then it will be blessed. In Israel's history the psalm most certainly refers to Israel and not yet to other nations.

We notice, too, the power ascribed to Yahweh—nothing happens without Yahweh's knowledge. Yahweh . . . brings, sees, frustrates, looks down, watches, and so on. These verbs reveal Israel's God to be active and attentive to God's people.

Psalm 33 is a powerful statement of faith. If we look especially at the last three verses (20-22), we see many of Jesus' New Testament themes foreshadowed by the psalmist: trust, steadfast love, and hope. Connections between Israel's faith and the church's are not as strained as we sometimes think. This faith is reflected in Augustine's observation of the human heart, which seems true for those having a religious heart: "Thou madest us for Thyself, and our heart is restless, until it repose in Thee."

* * *

Trust is a difficult stance for humans to develop. It seems in life we often have either too much trust or not enough. An eighteenth-century English proverb puts it, "It is an equal failing to trust everybody, and to trust nobody." But our psalm speaks not of trusting other human beings, nor does it speak of trusting human institutions. Rather, the psalm speaks of trusting God.

In today's lesson from Judges, one can only imagine what Gideon would have thought when the Lord instructed him to whittle down the size of his army. Common sense dictates that the more persons who are fighting on your side the better your chances of victory. Yet, several times the Lord tells Gideon, "These troops must return home."

According to the story, however, Israel's success was not due to the size of its army, but rather in spite of its size. Israel had the Lord of Hosts on its side. Israel was victorious because of its great trust in Yahweh.

Several years ago, there was a popular film about a successful underdog defeating a mighty opponent, called *The Karate Kid*. In this film, a young boy was given many tasks that made no sense to him. Putting wax on a car with certain prescribed hand motions and taking the wax off with another set of prescribed hand motions was especially irritating. The youngster, of course, could not see the point in such exacting methods, which were forced on him with no deviation allowed whatsoever.

Later, however, he understood that every motion he had learned would prove to be the exact motion necessary to master the art of karate. The exactness of the teacher made the student a superb practitioner even though, at the time, the exactness seemed to be nothing but a mindless chore. In order to learn, we often need to suspend our judgment, following the master's instruction. Most adults will follow a skilled, competent leader because they know that at times we must come to trust those who lead us.

All people must have an ultimate force in which to place trust. For Gideon and the psalmist, this ultimate force was God. Many people think that God would neither choose nor empower them. But God created people to be in fellowship with God and others. God chooses us because God wants us to be part of God's realm, created through Jesus Christ. When we come to terms with this "God wants even us," then we are on the way to trust.

Let us pray:
God of goodness and surprise, help us to accept the gift of grace you have given us in Jesus Christ. May we have the faith to trust in this world as you prepare us for the next. In Christ's name we pray. Amen.

October 16, 1994
READ IN YOUR BIBLE: Psalm 47
SUGGESTED PSALM: Same
SUGGESTED HYMN: A Mighty Fortress Is Our God (all)
　　　　　　　　Lead On, O King Eternal (B, C, E, F, L, P, UM)

Accepting Responsibility

This psalm is one of many psalms used by Israel to enthrone its king, making it a good companion for today's story of Israel's asking Samuel for a king. The psalm, however, is a positive assessment of Yahweh's kingship over Israel, while 1 Samuel 8 alludes to Israel's future and Israel's failure with human kings.

The beginning verses of this psalm call all people, but especially Israel, to worship the Lord—the Most High. Two reasons are given for the call to worship. First, this God subdued the nations around Israel. That is, the Lord protected Israel from its enemies. This God has universal power. Second, the psalmist says, "He chose our heritage for us," reflecting the peculiar covenant relationship Yahweh has with Israel. Israel is directed by Yahweh's choice.

We see an ironic twist when we place the stories from 1 Samuel next to the psalm. In the former, the people demand a king from Samuel. They want to choose for themselves, rather than let Yahweh chose for them, as Psalm 47 so powerfully counsels.

Indeed, the stories from 1 Samuel 8 and Psalm 47 mark the two alternatives always before Israel in choosing leadership for itself. One option is to "be like other nations," while the other is to be a peculiar and chosen people of God. The choice is clear, but responsibility is attached to the choice Israel makes. As the choice follows Israel, so will all people's choices. Perhaps, this is why our decisions are so crucial.

* * *

Accepting responsibility as a leader for God is to become a leader who is willing to lead all the people. "When everyone is in charge," the old saying goes, "then no one is in charge."

I have a pastor friend who for many years was lured into responding to each criticism he encountered. It is a good thing, I suppose, to heed criticism and use details that help one's ministry and life. But my friend, hyper-sensitive to criticism, lost his leadership perspective.

For instance, once a person complained the offering should not be placed on the altar because it was holy and of God. "Filthy lucre" should not have contact with a sacred place—the church's altar. So my friend instructed the ushers to position the offering plates on small flower tables near the altar.

After several weeks, the chair of my friend's finance committee said, "Pastor, I think we need to put our offering directly on the altar. If it represents our first fruits, then we should not be ashamed to place it there." My friend responded by putting one plate on the altar and the other on the side table.

Someone in that church loved my friend and took him aside, saying, "You are our leader and can make decisions. In fact, if you try to do as everyone suggests, soon people will lose respect for you because leaders understand their followers, but they do not always take directions from them." The wise person who told my friend this knew many adults look for leaders who will fulfill all their expectations. At the same time, leaders must also accept responsibility for the direction of those being led. In the church, leadership is under the guidance of God.

Today in politics we hear criticism of special interests, but special interests always operate in any community. Even in the family, we all have agendas that we want accepted. That is why good leaders in Israel, sometimes kings, sometimes prophets, always put the whole people's needs at the forefront of any decision made. Decisions for the good of the whole, not just certain groups, distinguished Israel's good leaders. Yahweh was suited to govern Israel, for Yahweh loved all the people. Yet, the people insisted on a king.

Good leaders put the needs of the whole community of faith before their own personal agenda. This is the mark of a faithful leader who knows how to accept godly responsibility.
Let us pray:

Lord, you understand how self-centered we can be and how possessive of the church's ministry we can become after years of service. Make us faithful to your tasks and mission for the world. Help us to remember that the church is of God and is not our own creation. Amen.

October 23, 1994

READ IN YOUR BIBLE: Psalm 106:40-48
SUGGESTED PSALM: 106: 1-11; 40-48
SUGGESTED HYMN: Dear Lord and Father of Mankind (B, C, E, F, L, P, UM)
Take Up Thy Cross (B, E, L, P, UM, W)

Overcoming Reluctance to Lead

Psalm 106 is a story, or history, of the salvation of Israel. It depicts cycles of Israel's faithfulness—sometimes steadfast, most often vacillating. Our verses, 40-48, complete the psalm with three distinct themes.

The first of the three sections expresses Yahweh's anger kindled against Israel. The background is the chosen people's apostasy occurring over and over again. In a very few verses the "old, old story" of Israel is recounted: The Lord gives them into the hand of their enemies, they are oppressed, and they hope for deliverance, even though they revel in rebellion.

The second section, introduced at verse 44, begins with the word *nevertheless*. It continues a thought from the previous verses, but holds a surprise. Even though our common sense might say of Yahweh "once burned, your fault; twice burned, my fault," this God of Israel is compassionate beyond measure. Yahweh restores Israel: "For their sake he remembered the covenant." The rainbow in Genesis 9 reminds Yahweh, not necessarily the people, of Yahweh's covenant.

The final section is both a prayer for deliverance and a prayer of praise for God's mercy. The deliverance reads as if it could have been issued during the Babylonian exile: "Gather us from among the nations." The praise is for God's everlasting salvation of God's people.

* * *

Many churches are now engaged in systematic, long-term Bible studies. There is a new and profound hunger for learning the Bible among church folk. I have taught a particular Bible study called *Disciple* for five years. In each class, about ten weeks into the study comes a question from a perplexed student. In the week dealing with Amos's assault on the royal household, a student will ask, "Why are we studying the Bible in this way?"

When I ask them to clarify their statement, they frankly admit that they came to be told by the preacher/teacher what these scripture texts signify—not to wrestle themselves with the meaning of the texts. But the *Disciple Bible Study* has a subliminal motive which is stated in its subtitle: *Becoming Disciples Through Bible Study*. The gospel's truth is that we Christians have been given scripture not only to feed upon, but to share with others who are hungering and thirsting for righteousness.

Many adults look to leaders who seem to have a sense of purpose. The startling thing for many Christians, not accustomed to thinking of themselves as leaders, is that by virtue of baptism they are "called out" by God. They are gospel ministers, expected to share the good news they have received by grace through faith. This is why, in my judgment, the *Disciple Bible Study* is devoted to its purpose: making disciples. Wasn't it Jesus, the risen Christ, who charged the disciples, as he withdrew from them in Matthew's Gospel, to go make more disciples?

Disciples are leaders because the purposes of God have converted them. There is no ducking this sacred call. Like Saul, we too may hide in our own baggage, but sooner or later, the Lord will have tasks of ministry for us. It is for this purpose that we have been bought with a price. Those persons who come to understand this and accept discipleship will be true carriers of the gospel.

Many of us fear taking on new responsibilities. Some feel worn down with other duties; others feel unworthy. It is by grace, however, that human beings do God's bidding. Saul was promised by Samuel, "The LORD has anointed you ruler over his people Israel" (1 Samuel 10:1). If we, today, could understand our ministries as sacred callings from God and God's church, think what renewed confidence of purpose we would possess. In every generation, people's overcoming the reluctance to lead is preceded by a divine call in perfect love, which casts out fear.

Let us pray:

Almighty God, our greatest weakness is in the strength of our fear of trusting you and surrendering to the tasks you have given us. Strengthen our resolve to become disciples in every aspect of our lives. In Christ's holy name, we pray. Amen.

October 30, 1994

READ IN YOUR BIBLE: 1 Samuel 15:22-26
SUGGESTED PSALM: Psalm 77:1-10
SUGGESTED HYMN: Jesus Calls Us O'er the Tumult (B, C, E, F, L, UM)
Hope of the World (E, L, P, UM, W)

Consequences of Disobedience

This text tells of a tragic beginning to Israel's monarchy. Today we may feel empathy for Saul, but understand the severity of Samuel. Specific sacrifice instructions were given to Saul by Samuel before an important military battle. Saul waits the time prescribed by Samuel to sacrifice, but the time comes and passes. The troops begin to desert Saul, and he must act. Saul was caught between two difficult choices, either spelling disaster.

Two previous verses sum up Saul's dilemma: "Samuel said, 'What have you done?' Saul replied, 'When I saw that the people were slipping away from me, and that you did not come within the days appointed, and that the Philistines were mustering at Michmash, I said, "Now the Philistines will come down upon me at Gilgal, and I have not entreated the favor of the LORD" so I forced myself, and offered the burnt offering'" (1 Samuel 13:11-12).

On commonsense grounds we can see why Saul made his choice. Samuel, however, asks some deeply penetrating questions when he suggests that obedience is more important than sacrifice; rebellion as sinful as divination.

The weight of biblical history judges Saul guilty. At least one lesson in our story today is that when we retain our authority to choose for ourselves, we must be careful, for choices are often more difficult than they appear. Saul found this out too late.

* * *

We all know people who leap before they look. We even know some who look, think twice about what they see, but leap anyway. Many adults have acted against their better judgment and later reaped the consequences. Each of us has stories in our past of disobedience and later paying a dear price.

One December, over a decade ago, my brother and I completed our school semester in Dallas and made ready for the thirty-six-hour car trip to Bakersfield, California. Before we left, we called our father to share our plans. As we said good-bye, he said clearly and distinctly to each of us, "Do not drive straight through!"

The next morning, we were feeling good in El Paso and decided to drive straight through. To this day, I'm not sure we would have tried to drive straight through if our father had not forbade it, but, perhaps, this is the nature of disobedience.

Outside Benson, Arizona, at daybreak, I was asleep, but so was my brother—and he was driving. We rolled over in our car several times, but it was so tightly packed and we had been going so slowly that neither one of us was hurt. We flipped a coin to see who had the honor of calling Father. I lost.

I spent that day—my birthday—in an Arizona wrecking yard. The dispatcher got a birthday cake, and we all had a birthday party as strangers became friends. But my brother and I learned an important lesson that day. Flouting authority is dangerous.

Every person eventually comes to terms with a higher authority in life. Whether it be parents, teachers, supervisors, or even God, there comes a time when we must trust those who have more experience and insight than we do. If we do not come to this understanding in human relationships, then we will always have trouble dealing with other people.

Saul, after a scathing confrontation with Samuel, confessed his sin. It was, however, too late. The course of Israel's history and the monarchy had already been set. David's star would soon rise, as well as that of Israel's. But Saul dies a tragic death, after living a tragic life. He dies, as predicted, after being badly wounded by some Philistine archers. Saul begs his armor-bearer to kill him, but when he refuses, Saul takes his own life. This is no way for Israel's king to die, but it is a consequence, so it seems, of bad decisions made long before.

Let us pray:
O God, you provide everything necessary for a full and meaningful life. You also give us the freedom to make decisions that affect many lives. They have consequences. Guide us by your Spirit. In Christ's name we pray. Amen.

November 6, 1994

READ IN YOUR BIBLE: Psalm 86:1-12
SUGGESTED PSALM: Psalm 86
SUGGESTED HYMNS: Just as I Am (B, C, E, F, L, P, UM)
　　　　　　　　Holy God, We Praise Thy Name (E, F, L, P, UM, W)

Claiming God's Promise

David wrote Psalm 86. It calls for deliverance from enemies. Three things impress us as noteworthy in this psalm: David's confidence in Yahweh, David's sense of despair, David's willingness to call on Yahweh.

Many phrases in this psalm reflect David's confidence in Yahweh. Especially illustrative of his confidence is verse 5: "For you, O LORD, are good and forgiving, /abounding in steadfast love to all who call on you." And verse 7 reads, "In the day of my trouble I call on you, /for you will answer me." In David's many moments of crisis, one thing never forsaken is his abundant confidence in Yahweh. We also note that Yahweh has confidence in David, too.

A second striking feature of this psalm is David's sense of despair. Although David has exceptional confidence in Yahweh, David also knows the human need out of which he calls on Yahweh. In David's reign, emergency after emergency occurs, yet he says: "I am poor and needy" and "in the day of my trouble."

Last, David's willingness to call on Yahweh is reflected at every point of the psalm. David's faith moves beyond the theoretical to the practical: "Teach me your way, O LORD, /that I may walk in your truth; /give me an undivided heart to revere your name." The gift of God can be accepted by any who have faith in God, know their human need, and willingly call on God.

* * *

Some adults have difficulty accepting gifts. This would seem to be an oddity in our consumer culture. Rather, it seems everyone is out to get something for nothing. When my state began the lottery, I realized my local convenience store was no longer convenient. It was jammed with lotto players. I never thought it would come to this: The bigger the jackpot, the longer it takes to pick up a gallon of milk on the way home from work.

Nonetheless, even in our consumer society, some adults have difficulty accepting gifts. Gifts symbolize relationships between giver and receiver. When I was in high school algebra, I was tutored by a young woman. I went to her parent's home once a week for instruction. She did not have a pencil sharpener and we usually needed one. Being practically oriented, I gave her a pencil sharpener for a Christmas gift and as a way to thank her.

Later, I discovered the gift upset her, because she thought we were dating—to which I had never given a moment's thought. For me the gift was just a gift, but for her it represented rejection. Gifts can carry unintended meanings.

David never had a problem asking God for anything. He and Yahweh had a long, close relationship. Although David's actions were not always righteous, the Bible portrays him as righteous in his heart toward Yahweh. This is why he could pray for Yahweh to "lift up the house of David forever."

Intercessory prayer—the kind of prayer many people use when they or someone else feels in trouble—must be based on a good relationship with God. If our praying is a hit-and-miss undertaking, based only on our needs and not a deeper relationship with God, then our prayer life looks like begging and is presumptuous. Many adults don't pray because they sense their prayer presumption and have not yet developed the deeper relationship necessary for authentic prayer.

The underlying and grace-filled truth about God, however, is that relationship with God is always given as a gift. We can never deserve it. We can only accept the gift of God's relationship as a gift we need, but don't deserve. As I read the story of David and try to feel the passion for Yahweh in his psalms, I sense that this passion was the vital center of who David was and from which he drew considerable strength.

To move toward David's model of faith, we would do well to reflect on his confidence and willingness to call on Yahweh.

Let us pray:
Lord, teach us to pray as a daily and constant reminder that, though we do not deserve your mercy and grace, we can never live well without it. Help us to accept your gift in Christ and be the people ever seeking your realm. Amen.

November 13, 1994

READ IN YOUR BIBLE: 1 John 1:5-10
SUGGESTED PSALM: Psalm 53
SUGGESTED HYMNS: O Gladsome Light (E, L, P, UM, W)
　　　　　　　　　Take My Life and Let It Be (B, C, E, L, P, UM, W)

Acknowledging Our Sin

If nothing else, the commonness of human sin is notable in Scripture. For instance, in John's Gospel, Jesus tells some accusers that those who are without sin should cast the first stone. All immediately leave. Paul, too, deals with the theme of universal sinfulness by saying that all people have sinned and fall short of the glory of God. The author of the epistle we call 1 John also takes up this theme.

Although it is probably more a sermon than a letter, 1 John has sage advice for the early church. Our verses have the common theme that all stand in need of the grace of God, for all walk in darkness without God. The teaching is that there are two kinds of persons. The first kind is a person of light, walking in God's light and by so doing having fellowship with God. The other kind of person is one walking in darkness, and though claiming fellowship with God, does "not do what is true."

This text speaks to every person's need to become children of light if they are to be true to God. Human beings, on the other hand, are creatures of the darkness, even though they deceive themselves with the self-perception of being children of light. In today's lesson in 2 Samuel, when David was confronted, and in a sense caught red-handed by Nathan, David had the integrity to openly confess his sin. In fact, no one can seriously claim to be without sin.

* * *

One of the cardinal elements in Christian belief is that people have no standing before God. This is what makes God, God and what makes people, people. When the line of demarcation between humanity and divinity blurs, then heresy is born, as when people aspire to be like gods. Satan's temptation of the man and woman in the garden is a useful illustration. The converse is also problematic, for when God becomes mysteriously incarnate in Christ, then interpretive heresies begin to proliferate. Our texts establish that God is absolutely just and is the light, in marked contrast to people.

Perhaps, one of the most embarrassing moments many of us face is when we try to forgive someone for something he or she feels no responsibility for at all. Often, when we do find ourselves in such a position, there will be great anger toward us.

I remember quite vividly a controversy one Sunday morning after our worship service. It concerned something I had said in the worship service preparing to serve the Lord's Supper. I had quoted Psalm 51:5, "Indeed, I was born guilty, /a sinner when my mother conceived me," as a prayer of confession before the words of forgiveness were pronounced. I had paraphrased it in the biblical words of an older translation, "in sin did my mother conceive me." A young man angrily confronted me by saying, "Don't you ever say anything like that about my mom again!"

Later, I took the opportunity to teach the doctrine of original sin and how all people participate in it. The use of "mothers" is simply a poetic way of saying "all people." Every time humans gather to worship, they underline the difference between them and God and, therefore, reassert their dependence on God by their confession of sin. If sin is separation from God, as much as little acts that reflect separation, then we are all guilty—exactly the Bible's point.

Most adults have a sense of fairness regarding others. Most of us try to give others the benefit of the doubt. In spite of this, those who have been saved by God, through faith in Christ, are reminded what the Bible constantly tells us. We are a fallen people, for if we were not, then there would be no necessity for a savior. First John 1:9 says: "If we confess our sins, he who is faithful and just will forgive us our sins and cleanse us from all unrighteousness." In order to receive the full benefits of Christ's Passion, we must see our need of forgiveness.

Let us pray:
Forgiving God, you have done for us what we cannot do for ourselves. You have forgiven us in your Son Christ Jesus. Make us holy and pure in Christ's name. Amen.

November 20, 1994

READ IN YOUR BIBLE: Proverbs 3:5-15
SUGGESTED PSALM: Psalm 49
SUGGESTED HYMNS: Holy God, We Praise Thy Name (E, F, L, P, UM, W)
                        He Leadeth Me (B, C, F, L, UM)

Living Wisely

Today's devotional text gives us biblical counsel regarding human behavior that leads wise people to prosperity. The last part of the Proverbs passage extols the general virtues of wisdom. Our background scripture is yoked to the devotional passage by the idea of wisdom. Proverbs speaks about wisdom's goodness, while Solomon embodies wisdom's virtue through various biblical accounts and later legends.

A proverb is a short descriptive sentence containing a commonly held truth. Many of the world's religions have proverbs, and they are good to use with youngsters because they are easily remembered. Although Jesus often used proverbs in his teaching, he did not always so note them as he did in Luke 4:23: "Doubtless you will quote to me this proverb, 'Doctor, cure yourself!' And you will say, 'Do here also in your hometown the things that we have heard you did at Capernaum.' "

Proverbs 3:5-12 is sprinkled with value-charged words that are as esteemed in our culture as they were in the Hebrew culture. We see loyalty, faithfulness, trust, and honor as among those virtues for which human beings should strive.

The final three verses of our devotional text speak about how one will be made "happy" or "blessed" by living according to the precepts of wisdom. Wisdom is more precious than jewels, and long life may be granted by wisdom. In the Hebrew tradition wisdom is often elevated to the common sense one secures by faithfulness to Yahweh and Yahweh's law.

* * *

Steven Covey's *Seven Habits of Highly Effective People* does for our decade what Proverbs has done for 2,000 years for Christians and longer for Judaism's faithful. Many people have read Covey's book and raved about its helpfulness in focusing their lives. Habit number five is a good representative of the others.

It says, "Seek first to understand, then to be understood." This statement reflects to a close degree St. Francis's prayer: "O Divine Master, grant that I may not so much seek . . . to be understood, as to understand."

What this means is simply that for people to best connect with others, they must first come to a genuine awareness of others. This interest in others is what leads people to true prosperity, of which our Proverbs speak—it is not simply economic prosperity, either. The best salespeople are those who think of their customers as more than mere consumers. My insurance agent knows my children's names and has always had a genuine interest in my family. Even before he became a salesperson, we knew him as a man. And he knew us. This is why we buy insurance from him. It is difficult for people to feign genuine interest in others.

Proverbs puts Judaism's wisdom into short and memorable sayings. When Proverbs 1:5-6 says, "Let the wise also hear and gain in learning, and the discerning acquire skill, to understand a proverb and a figure, the words of the wise and their riddles" it suggests those who are wise learn from the proverbs.

Many adults desire to use their life to make a positive difference. Steven Covey and Dale Carnegie before him have tried to help people understand the wisdom of working on our lives and our relationships with others in order to make a positive difference. Proverbs long ago did this, but made it explicit that the truly wise gain wisdom from Yahweh.

Several years ago a football player, Gale Sayers, wrote a book, *I Am Third*. In it he made a simple case that if people would put God first, others second, and themselves third many problems people encountered would be quickly resolved. This book was roundly criticized for being too simplistic, but in our sophisticated world, perhaps it is worth remembering. The only life worth living is the life given away in loving concern for others.

Let us pray:
O God of the living and the dead, make us understand that to trust in you alone is the freedom we seek. Allow us to so give ourselves to others that people will see Christ's love in us and through us. We ask this and every prayer in the name of Jesus Christ. Amen.

November 27, 1994

READ IN YOUR BIBLE: Proverbs 16:1-7
SUGGESTED PSALM: Psalm 65
SUGGESTED HYMNS: Hope of the World (L, P, UM, W)
        Jesus Shall Reign (all)

Turning Away from God

First Kings 11 begins telling the story of the monarchy's end of a united Israel under Solomon. The texts make amply clear that Solomon, because of his 700 foreign wives and 300 foreign concubines, began to turn from the Lord. A legal proscription of the day was that Israelites could not marry persons of other nationalities because of the foreign religious and cultural influences brought by these foreigners.

The book of Proverbs was a collection of maxims teaching Israelites right principles by which to live. Generally, we could say Proverbs was a theological justification of Israel's common sense given in short sayings.

Proverbs 16 contains sayings that compare and contrast the plans and ways of mortals to the plan and way of the Lord. It teaches that if we are faithful to Yahweh, then we will surely prosper in life. This idea of prosperity includes not only economic prosperity, but also the whole scope of human life. These other signs of prosperity, health, and happiness for instance, disclose God's favor.

In fact, a majority of the "wisdom writings" (Psalms, Proverbs, Ecclesiastes) understand prosperity as a reward for faithfulness to Yahweh. Job, a wisdom book written to counteract this theology, asks: Why do the innocent suffer? The balance of wisdom theology can be summed up by Proverbs 16:7, "When the ways of people please the LORD, /he causes even their enemies to be at peace with them."

* * *

The Christian faith calls people out of the world and into a relationship with God through Jesus Christ. It is true that often the Bible will use the term *world* in a positive sense, for instance, "For God so loved the world that he gave his only Son" (John 3:16). But often *world* is used to describe that from which saved people are to escape. For instance, John 7:7 reads, "The world cannot hate you, but it hates me because I testify against it that its works are evil."

People are influenced by their local and world cultures. We are influenced as young children by our parents and siblings. As we mature, however, we are influenced to a greater and greater extent by others. Every parent knows the struggle: trying to teach children that sometimes what other people do and say is not acceptable in our homes. This is the world at work on our meaning-making and values. Proverbs teaches people of faith to come to terms with faith's requirements opposed to the expectations of the world. As Solomon's life is an all too clear illustration, even children from the best homes can fall away.

I read an ancient rabbi's story that helped to put into perspective my responsibility within God's world. Once there was master who hired a carpenter to build a house while he went to a far country on business. He gave the carpenter an open account to acquire materials and pay workers to construct the house. The carpenter, however, was shrewd and thought this was a good opportunity to make a quick and handsome profit. So he hired cheap laborers, purchased inferior building materials, and built the house as expediently as possible, with no thought about quality. All flaws were covered with paint.

Months later, the master of the household returned home and received the keys to the house. Returning them to the carpenter, he said, "I hope you have built well, because I give you this house you built as a gift. You may live in it until you die."

We live in a culture that tells us to look out for ourselves and do it to others before they do it to us. The Bible, however, has another ethic. It shows us a more excellent way. Our Scripture tells us that our faith in God is all the security we will ever need and that our relationship with others and our God is the single most important factor in human existence. "Commit your work to the LORD, /and your plans will be established" (Proverbs 16:3).

Let us pray:
O God, all we have is from your gracious hand. Help us to trust your promises, which have come to us in the lives of the saints and in our Scripture. In Christ's name we pray, amen.

December 4, 1994
READ IN YOUR BIBLE: Isaiah 40:3-11
SUGGESTED PSALM: Psalm 114
SUGGESTED HYMNS: Near to the Heart of God (B, C, F, P, UM)
Holy God, We Praise Thy Name (E, F, L, P, UM, W)

Prepare for a New Life

In chapters 1—39, Isaiah warned the Israelites that destruction was coming because of their sin and lack of concern for justice. Then, in the silence between chapters 39 and 40, the prophet's words came true. Babylon, a mighty foreign power, crushed the Southern Kingdom of Judah. This area included Jerusalem, and the Temple there was utterly destroyed. Many people were killed, and most others were forced to live far from their homes in the bitter event known as the Exile. But instead of saying "I told you so," the prophet offers hope to the exiles in chapters 40-55.

The images of wilderness in today's devotional reading would have reminded the Jewish exiles of the wanderings of their ancestors in the desert in the time of Moses. In the desert of the Exile, like the wilderness experienced by their ancestors, the Israelites were called to prepare for new life in the promised land. This "desert" is more than literal—it also stands for the dry, lifeless condition of the soul; the absence of vibrant new life. The message of this passage to a sinful, suffering community is to prepare their hearts and lives; despite their past mistakes, God has great plans for new life.

In the same way, John the Baptist, who also dwelled in the desert, challenged his contemporaries to prepare for a new life, to prepare their hearts for the coming of Christ.

* * *

For $1.75, my family got a package of five pumpkin seeds. These were no ordinary seeds, however; the catalog boasted that individual pumpkins could grow up to 500 pounds. Understandably, the kids were delighted when the seeds came in the mail, so we selected a secluded spot near the fence and began to prepare a plot for the precious seeds. The ground was hard, so we turned it over and over, breaking up the clods with our hands and mixing in peat moss. Finally we made mounds and placed a seed in each.

As of this writing the pumpkin plants have come up and are growing larger each day in their moist, fertile soil. The pumpkins have not yet begun to form on the lengthening vines, but I am confident that someday they will. What I am less confident about is figuring out a way to move, much less carve, a 500-pound pumpkin! But that will be October's problem—how to deal with such abundance.

Meanwhile, the situation in the pumpkin patch is symbolic. Like the Israelites and John the Baptist's audience, our sin makes our hearts like stone-hard ground. The homeless sleep on the streets right in front of the locked doors of the church. The poor cannot afford as much "equal justice under the law" as the rich can. When disaster strikes a poor area of a city, people there do not receive help as quickly and completely as disasters that demolish the homes and businesses of the wealthy. Our sin is a national and personal disaster, wreaking consequences on our morals, our children, and our faith. So today, just as in Isaiah's day and John the Baptist's day, God is calling us to prepare for new life in the future.

The pumpkins are growing so well because the seeds were placed in fertile, loose soil. When we prepare our hearts for the coming of the Lord, then God's seeds of love, forgiveness, and hope will grow as fast as a pumpkin vine. We cannot see the future with certainty, but we can know in faith that it will be abundant, like looking at the growing pumpkin vines and seeing in our heart the coming day of the 500 pounders.

The challenge of preparation is to leave the sins of the past behind us and to make fertile soil for the seeds of God's kingdom—right in our own backyard.

Let us pray:

Dear Lord, help us to discern both our spiritual disasters of deserting your way and the seeds of hope you have scattered in our lives. Today we recommit ourselves to the sacred task of preparation. We ask you to level the mountains of our sin and fill in the valleys of our lack of faith. Prepare in us a smooth path, that we may walk with you into the bright future you have prepared for us. Amen.

December 11, 1994

READ IN YOUR BIBLE: John 1:1-14
SUGGESTED PSALM: Psalm 119:105-112
SUGGESTED HYMNS: Lo, a Rose E'er Blooming (B, E, F, L, P, UM, W)
O Little Town of Bethlehem (all)

Hold On to Your Faith

John 1:1-18, known as the "Prologue" to the Gospel of John, differs from the beginnings of the other three Gospels. Matthew and Luke begin with the preparation for and birth of Jesus. Mark omits Jesus' birth and simply begins with the ministry of John the Baptist as an adult. But only the Gospel of John includes this cryptic "prologue." What does it mean? What is it saying about Jesus?

The first sentence says that Jesus, "The Word," is one with God; therefore, the beginnings of Jesus are not found only in Bethlehem. Rather, Jesus is eternal just as God is eternal—for Jesus and God are inseparable. Like God, Jesus was there for the creation of the world as well as the thirty-three years he spent "dwelling among us" in the world.

John, the latest Gospel written, shows in this prologue the beginnings of Christian thought about the Trinity—God the Father, God the Son, and God the Holy Spirit—three "persons," yet one and the same God.

The Gospel of John also makes heavy use of the images of light and darkness, and the associated images of blindness (darkness) and sight or perception (light). In the prologue, some people failed to "see the light" (which shines on everyone), in spite of the work of John the Baptist, who spoke about the light. Even John the Baptist, from the "darkness" of his prison cell, sent a message asking Jesus if he really was the Messiah. However, the prologue points out that God's children "see the light" and believe.

* * *

Many children (and some adults, too) are afraid of the dark and lose their sense of security when the lights go out. Parents of these children often put "night lights" in their rooms. It is interesting that many night lights are the size that accomodate bulbs designed for Christmas tree lights. There is something about seeing the glow of colorful Christmas tree lights in a darkened room that lifts our hearts and reminds us to keep our faith alive. In the same way there is something about one small light in a dark room that keeps a young child from panicking in the darkness.

If electricity had been invented in biblical times, the night light might have become a symbol of the faith. Certainly Jesus would have been tempted to compare Christians to "night lights" when he said, "You are the light of the world" (Matthew 5:14). For the world can be a dark place, and in need of "light." Jesus, the light of the world, says that we must also be light for the world.

A teen hangs up the phone after her boyfriend breaks up with her. A man leaves the hospital stunned by the news that he is now a widower. A woman loses her job. A patient hears a bad prognosis. A child cannot understand why Mommy and Daddy fight and want to live apart. One country bombs another. Floods wash away a lifelong home, and people die on the sidewalk in the winter, homeless in the midst of an affluent society. These things can cause us to question our faith, just as John the Baptist wondered about Jesus while he was in prison.

Night lights are not a substitute for a 60-watt bulb in a ceiling light. Instead, they are like an exception to the darkness, a reminder that a brighter light exists. In this way they help us hold on to our faith in the light.

In response to John the Baptist's question in Matthew 11, Jesus pointed to the acts of healing he had done, which point to a greater light. Being a Christian is a matter of "glowing" in the midst of darkness like a night light, witnessing to the fact that Jesus is the light of the world.

Let us pray:
O God of light, your first words during the days of creation were "Let there be light." We rejoice to recognize the light of the world in Jesus, who heals our spiritual blindness and helps us to see your purpose for us. Help us to witness to the hope and joy of this light, so that through us others might come to know you and serve you. This we pray through Jesus Christ, the light of our life. Amen.

December 18, 1994

READ IN YOUR BIBLE: Isaiah 9:2-7
SUGGESTED PSALM: Psalm 4
SUGGESTED HYMNS: O Come, O Come, Emmanuel (B, E, F, L, P, UM, W)
O Come, All Ye Faithful (all)

Jesus Is Born

Before you read Isaiah 9:2-7, read Isaiah 8:21-22. It is easier to understand the significance of the vision of the light in Isaiah 9 if you have first appreciated the darkness in Isaiah 8. The historical situation of Isaiah 1–39 is the dark period before Babylon conquered Judah, the Southern Kingdom of the Jewish people (which contained the Jewish Temple in Jerusalem).

These were "dark" days for the prophet Isaiah and the Israelite people, not only because of the obvious fear that might occur due to the threat of being conquered by a much larger, hostile country, but also because the people were giving up their faith. They were turning to other religions for answers and help in their time of need; they turned their back on their king and on their God.

Into this situation Isaiah spoke these words about light shining on the people who walked in darkness, and about rejoicing over the birth of a king who would be like King David. King David ruled the Israelites during the greatest time in their history, so it was natural for them to hope for another king like David. Centuries later, Matthew sees in Jesus' birth the fulfillment of these words. Christians see in Jesus' birth "Emmanuel," God with us.

* * *

We already know that "Emmanual" means "God is with us." By that we usually mean that we were here on this earth, and then God came here to be with us in the form of Jesus Christ. Thus in this way of thinking the birth of Jesus means that God moved a little closer to us.

However, an old story might add a second dimension to that line of thinking, as does today's scripture. The story features an older couple riding down the road peacefully. Suddenly the woman turns to her husband, who is driving, and says part wistfully, part accusingly, "You know, years ago we used to ride down the road sitting right next to each other. You used to put your arm around me, and we cuddled as we traveled." The man rode on in silence for a while, then answered, "Honey, I ain't the one who moved." ~~If you were going to use this story in a sermon, you might point out that~~ God is still there for us, and it is we who have moved.

Even before Jesus was born, the Israelites had a habit of moving away from God. In fact, that is not a problem unique to the ancient Israelites. Christians today know that God is with us, but often we do not choose to be with God. So when we feel distant, we are the ones who have moved.

The fact is that humans have never consistently "cozied up" to God. When we are riding down the road with God, pouting at the opposite end of the seat is often a fitting picture of us. We have to discipline ourselves to pray and read the Bible (because we are reluctant to draw near to God without forcing ourselves to do it). Jesus pointed out that many of us have loved the darkness more than the light; as a result, we often dwell in a self-imposed darkness.

Christianity is unique among all the world's religions. In other faiths, gods are pictured as ruling from far away. At best they send teachers and messengers to their people. Sometimes they are reported to call a follower to them. Our God is the only one who comes to his people. It looks demeaning for a god, but it is a sign of our God's love for his people.

The meaning, and the miracle, of "God with us" is that in spite of our reluctance to draw near to God, "while we were sinners Christ died for us" (Romans 5:8). We were God's enemies, but he made us his friends." *Emmanuel* means that with or without our willingness to draw near to God, God has made a decision to be with us where we are, as we are. Thanks be to God!

Let us pray:
Sometimes, Lord, when we pray we ask you to be with us, although we know through the birth of Jesus that you have always been there. Now we pray that you will help us to truly be with you as we live our lives from this day forward. Amen.

December 25, 1994
READ IN YOUR BIBLE: Isaiah 11:1-9
SUGGESTED PSALM: Psalm 97
SUGGESTED HYMNS: Silent Night (all)
                    Joy to the World (B, C, E, F, L, P, UM, W)

God's Great Gift

This treasured scripture passage pictures a kingdom filled with such righteousness and peace that even animals that we know as enemies would lie down together without fear. However, the world in which this passage was written was far from peaceful. It is interesting to read between the lines, remembering that to say "He will rule his people with justice and integrity" (v. 5) implies that current leaders are unjust and lack integrity.

Because of their unfaithfulness to God, Isaiah pictures the people of Israel as a tree that has been cut down, and in the preceding verses, Assyria is compared to the Lord's axe. Assyria was the mighty country that conquered the Northern Kingdom and still threatened the Southern Kingdom, which contained Jerusalem. (To better understand this, read Isaiah 10, particularly vv. 13-15, 20-23, and 28-34.)

This message, and the image of the tree that has been cut down, would not have been missed by Israelites of Isaiah's day. This passage, beautiful as it is, is still essentially a criticism (by comparison with a better ideal) of the lack of faith and commitment to the Lord, which was evident in Judah. Yet it also expresses confidence that God plans to carry on his purposes with a remnant, symbolized by the branches coming from the tree stump. (See also Isaiah 61:1-4, especially v. 3—words quoted by Jesus in Luke 4:16-20 to define his ministry.)

* * *

One Christmas evening during World War I, it is reported, a cease-fire fell with the darkness upon fighting American and German ground troops. The young men on both sides of the line had to spend that night dug into their foxholes. As the evening wore on, some of the American soldiers began to sing Christmas carols. While singing "Silent Night," they were shocked to hear the German soldiers join in. Throughout that night, soldiers on both sides sang many songs, sometimes together and sometimes to each other. As the morning light erased the stars and the magic of the moment, the fighting resumed.

Perhaps it is unrealistic to wish that a few songs could stop a conflict like World War I, especially when Jesus' own birth and subsequent life did not stop the enmity between his people and their oppressive Roman occupiers. Like Isaiah's vision of wolves and sheep living together in peace, it is a standard that seems hopelessly high. Yet the songs on the battlefield, like the moments in the stable long ago, offer us a glimpse of the way the world was meant to be, and in Christ, will one day become. These inspired moments, whether they occur on the battlefield or in a rocking chair holding our sleeping grandchild, are like an oasis of peace. They offer life-giving water in the midst of a desert of violence, racism, war, and hatred. They help us to know, as we leave the oasis behind and continue through the desert, that peace is not an impossible dream. The oasis is a much needed taste of the promised land, a place flowing with milk and honey, where lambs can lie down with lions, and swords are beat into plowshares, and nobody has to be afraid. The oasis seems to say that someday, with God's help, we'll get there. We just need to keep listening, across our fields of battle, to the guiding faith expressed in the song,

> Stille Nacht, heilige Nacht!
> Alles schläft, einsam wacht
> Nur das traute hochheilige Paar,
> Holder Knabe mit lockigem Haar,
> Schlaf im himmlischer Ruh, schlaf im himmlisher Ruh.

Let us pray:

Lord, on this Christmas morning, we humbly kneel in our hearts before the manger. We feel the hope, peace, and love you bring to the world. We ask you to dwell in our hearts today, and make there an oasis of peace. Grant that our work in this life will move all people toward that heavenly vision of peace you have given us. In the name of the Prince of Peace, Jesus Christ, I pray. Amen.

January 1, 1995
READ IN YOUR BIBLE: Luke 4:16-21
SUGGESTED PSALM: Psalm 84
SUGGESTED HYMNS: Go, Tell It on the Mountain (B, E, F, L, P, UM, W)
Just as I Am (B, C, E, F, L, P, UM)

Deliverance and Forgiveness

This passage makes plain the fact that Jesus regularly attended the synagogue on the Sabbath. Looking ahead to Luke 4:31, he is next pictured on the Sabbath in Capernaum's synagogue, a town in Galilee a few miles to the north. This event, however, takes place in his hometown synagogue in Nazareth. So the people there know his parents well and can remember Jesus as a baby, a teen, and a young carpenter. As was normal for a Sabbath in the synagogue, any layperson could read the scripture and preach about it. It was read standing (from one of the scrolls), and the "sermon" was delivered while sitting down. This time, however, the hometown young man selected Isaiah 61:1-2, a treasured prophecy about the future reign of God, and identified himself as being the fulfillment of it. What would you think if a grown-up youth from your church came home, read the Bible in church, and then said he was the fulfillment of it?

For Jesus, this passage beautifully described his mission in life, though it was predictable that those in his hometown had divided opinions about Jesus' sermon. The healings of the two men with demons and of the paralyzed man, which are part of our reading today in Matthew, vividly demonstrate the meaning and fulfillment of Isaiah 61:1-2 through Jesus' ministry.

* * *

A car in front of me at a stop light bore the license plate "Letmego." I looked at the driver, but she did not resemble Moses. I began to wonder why she wanted "Letmego" for her license plate, or whether it was perhaps a way for the convict in the state prison who had made it to voice a silent plea to the world. Then the light turned green, and those of us who had been held captive for those moments behind the red light were given our freedom to move on with the rest of our lives.

Whether it was the prisoner's idea or the car owner's to print "Letmego" on that license plate, it was made and mailed and mounted some time ago. And on this new day, as this is being written, that prisoner is probably still behind bars somewhere, waiting for freedom. If not him, then someone else is working in his place, sorting through the stack of license plate orders, silently praying for the day when he or she can experience freedom again. And the day will come, one way or another, for all prisoners. No person has ever been behind bars forever—perhaps for life—but not forever.

It is a little like sitting at a stop light, hemmed in by stopped cars on every side. We all experience little captivities, and sometimes big ones. Stop lights don't usually bother us when they hold us captive unless we are in a hurry and hit all of them. But being captive in an abusive relationship, or in a body that no longer does what it once did, or by a destructive habit that we long to break—these are more serious captivities. The most universal of all, of course, is sin. It grips us like a cat's claws; the harder we pull away, the deeper it digs in. At least a cat only clings to the surface. Sin has us by the soul, a prisoner to its demonic, ungodly urges. That is why our prayer, whether we are prisoner or we seem to hit all of life's green lights, needs to be "Letmego."

God's answer to our prayer, as captive people, is found in Jesus Christ. "The Spirit of the Lord is upon me. . . . He has sent me to proclaim release to the captives . . . to let the oppressed go free, to proclaim the year of the Lord's favor" (Luke 4:18-19). It does not matter whether our bonds of captivity are spiritual or physical. When suffering from constraints, we can always petition for release in prayer.

Let us pray:
When I feel trapped by my busy schedule or a lack of finances, O Lord, "Letmego." When I feel shackled by a tough relationship or bad feelings, "Letmego." When my soul is a prisoner to sin, please "Letmego," O Lord. Thank you for the freedom and new life you give me in Jesus' name. Amen.

January 8, 1995

READ IN YOUR BIBLE: Isaiah 42:1-9
SUGGESTED PSALM: Psalm 24:1-6
SUGGESTED HYMNS: What Wondrous Love Is This (B, E, F, L, P, UM,)
Lord, Speak to Me (B, C, F, L, P, UM)

A Leader Who Serves

For Jews, the word *servant* in this passage refers to the Jewish community as God's servant among the nations (see Isaiah 41:8), even though the pronouns are singular ("he"; "him"). Thus one purpose of Israel was to establish justice for all people and tell other nations that the Lord alone is God.

When Christians read Isaiah 42:1-8, it is natural to think of Jesus as the "servant" in this passage. This is reinforced by Matthew's interpretation of Isaiah in today's lesson (Matthew 12:15-21), which explains that Jesus' healings and ministry happened to fulfill Isaiah's prophecy in 42:1-4. When studying Isaiah 42:1-4, it is also important to realize that the first verse forms part of the words God spoke to Jesus from heaven at Jesus' baptism, "This is my Son, the Beloved, with whom I am well pleased" (Matthew 3:17). The same words come from the cloud at Jesus' Transfiguration experience (Matthew 17:5). These are key moments for Jesus, the first confirming the beginning of his public ministry, and the second confirming his decision to go to Jerusalem where he would die for all humanity. These moments help to define his role as a servant for humanity rather than a leader who is waited upon by others.

* * *

During the great Mississippi River flood of 1993, my family had the opportunity to spend part of a day filling sandbags in Pittsfield, Illinois, to help strenghthen the levees nearby. Filling sandbags is hot, backbreaking work; however, it is a tangible, hands-on way to serve persons facing catastrophe and needing all the help they can get. Most of the people who filled sandbags did not personally own any of the farms or homes that were threatened by the flood waters. Instead, at one point so many people came in buses from all over the Midwest that some actually had to be turned away.

The day I was there several strong teenage boys came to our pile to load up the bags my family and I had filled to that point. A pastor they apparently knew was standing nearby, laughing and talking with the people. Then he loudly accepted a glass of iced tea from someone there. One of the teens indignantly remarked as he threw our bags onto the truck, "Look at that preacher there. He thinks he's just too good to fill sandbags."

"Yeah!" replied another in disgust. "I guess all preachers are good for is praying."

The boys did not know I am a preacher, and so for a moment I was tempted to straighten up, wipe the sweat off my brow, and mention my line of work to them. However, I didn't want them to think preachers are also eavesdroppers, so I decided against defending my cleric brother at that time. Instead, my wife and I exchanged smiles and filled another sandbag.

The most effective leadership usually happens when leaders focus on serving the people rather than seeking to be served by them. Jesus did not expect the crowds to cater to his needs; instead, he actively went about healing the sick and serving those in need. As Isaiah suggested, he did not shout or make loud speeches in the streets, as an arrogant leader might. Instead, he simply sought to establish justice for everyone on the earth. He had tremendous power, but he used it to help people instead of helping himself. Jesus demonstrated this powerfully when he healed on the sabbath in Matthew 12; he was a leader who serves.

It is tempting for us to see our money, our time, our family, and our friends as one great big web of life that exists to support and serve us. But to follow Christ means that in the church, Christ's body, we see our money, our time, and our abilities as one great big web of life that exists to support and serve others.

Let us pray:

O Lord, help us to follow your perfect example of service. You went about helping the humble, the poor, and the sick without ever asking for payment or services for yourself. Forgive us, for we fall so short of your perfect service. Renew and strengthen us, that we may bend our backs for the good of others. In Jesus' name, amen.

January 15, 1995
READ IN YOUR BIBLE: Isaiah 35:5-10
SUGGESTED PSALM: Psalm 122
SUGGESTED HYMNS: My Faith Looks Up to Thee (B, C, E, F, L, P, UM)
                        Now Thank We All Our God (B, E, F, L, P, UM, W)

Persistent Faith

The words of Isaiah 35:1-10 appear to refer to the situation of the Exile, after the fall of Jerusalem. This is because they envision a time when the people will come back to Jerusalem, and presumably they would first have to be scattered in order to return there. However, this scenario does not neatly fit into Isaiah 1-39, since those chapters as a whole are prophecies before the fall of Judah, warning the people to turn back to the Lord (or else Judah will be destroyed at the hands of the Assyrians). Some scholars believe that this chapter really belongs with chapters 40-55, since it comes from the same historical situation, and seems to offer comfort to people who are already stricken.

In any case, these beautiful words give us an image of the kingdom of God. The effect of these words on the suffering person who reads them is to encourage faith and persistence in times of trouble, because God is going to change things for the better. For instance, physical problems will be cured (the blind see, the deaf hear, and the lame dance). Here we see a connection with Matthew 15:21-31 (Jesus' healing many people). Hostile elements of nature will be changed (fierce animals will not be present and deserts will be fertile places). Even the people are singing and shouting for joy—just as those who are praising the God who made this possible would be.

* * *

Friends of our family began to be concerned about the health of their six-week-old baby. There was no definitive symptom, but to the infant girl's mother, the baby cried more than expected and "just didn't seem right." She took her daughter to the doctor, who suggested that perhaps the child wasn't getting enough to eat. The anxious mother paid special attention to the child's nutrition. But the baby's general condition did not improve. Over the next several months, our friend took her little girl back to the doctor repeatedly, although the doctor resisted ordering expensive testing on the infant.

Between the ages of six months and one year the baby did not gain even one ounce. After the mother persistently insisted that the baby needed further tests, the doctor relented and ordered them. The diagnosis: liver cancer. The huge tumor was in the fourth stage, the fifth being inoperable and terminal. Fortunately, the baby's tumor was still treatable, and the girl, now in grade school, continues to be completely free of cancer after surgery and follow-up treatments.

Anyone who has children, and most people who don't, can imagine the anguish experienced by a parent with a desperately sick child. The Canaanite woman in this story is just such a person. Like our friends, she was very worried about her daughter, but she was also very persistent in seeking a cure for her. In spite of the disciples' antagonism and Jesus' initial reluctance to deal with her, this Canaanite woman refused to take for an answer "We have not been sent to help you."

We are repeatedly faced with problems, and it is important that we are as persistent in our faith and prayers to God as the problems are pesistent in arising. Isaiah 15:5-10 was written to encourage people with problems to keep their faith in God's ability to rescue them. Likewise, Matthew 15:21-28 encourages people with a problem, whether that means a sick child or some other difficulty in life, to be persistent in faith. It is difficult to understand Jesus' slowness to help this woman, knowing his personality and apparent willingness to heal everyone else who asked him for aid. But often we feel just like her, too. We sometimes feel that God is slow to answer our requests for help. It is then that this story has particular meaning and encouragement to offer. First be persistent in faith. But also be persistent in asking for help. God is still on our side.

Let us pray:
Dear Lord, we often expect too much from you. We ask a great deal and offer very little in return. Strengthen our faith, so that it may withstand the difficulties of life. And through our faith, strengthen us, that we may always stand with you. Amen.

January 22, 1995

READ IN YOUR BIBLE: 2 Peter 1:16-21
SUGGESTED PSALMS: Psalm 63
SUGGESTED HYMN: Break Thou the Bread of Life (B, C, F, L, P, UM)
　　　　　　　　O Morning Star, How Fair and Bright (E, L, P, UM, W)

Challenged to Hear

The second letter from Peter was written to early Christians (no one group in particular). In this letter he is concerned about false teachers (who make up stories), and today's passage reminds his readers of one of his credentials—he was an eyewitness of Christ's glory during Jesus' transfiguration (besides being a key disciple).

Peter's point in 1:16-21 is perhaps summarized by the second half of verse 19, "You will do well to be attentive to this [the message proclaimed by the prophets] as to a lamp shining in a dark place." Peter has heard the voice of God himself during the Transfiguration, and he challenges his readers to pay attention to God's voice as heard through the prophets. Verses 20-21 remind the reader that the prophets did not make up their stories either; they were under the control of the Holy Spirit as they spoke God's message.

* * *

One day I wanted some more tea near the end of the ladies' meeting at church, and Elizabeth, a sometimes gruff but humorous octogenarian, was getting some too. As we looked over the counter at the fifteen or so women in the room below us who were engaged in conversation, Elizabeth wryly commented with affectionate disgust, "Just look at them! Every one of them talking and not one of them listening!"

Besides striking a humorous chord in me, I still remember her comment for its deeper perception. There are not enough listeners in the world. When we talk, it is usually about ourselves or things we are interested in. But when we listen, we have to put another person's talk ahead of our own. That means putting someone else first, and for most of us it takes deliberate effort.

Real listening is never casual, like hearing the words "Time for dinner" and automatically saying "Okay" with our eyes still glued to the TV like a zombie. To listen to others, we must concentrate on their words and empathize with their feelings. Real listening is rare, even though it is one of the best ways to minister to the real needs of another person.

God certainly knows it is hard for people to pay attention (particularly to the right things), and so did Peter. Both of them apparently worried that people would not hear, or would hear and accept the wrong message uncritically. So both God and Peter gave a message that could be summarized, "Listen!" In the same way, liturgists in some churches say, just before they read the Scripture lessons, "Listen for the word of the Lord." It is a good reminder.

One wonders whether God might sometimes look at the people who gather at church meetings and observe, "Just look at them! Every one of them talking, and not one of them listening!" We bring our preprinted agendas to board meetings, and often to life too. Before Peter wised up on the mountaintop, he rebuked the Lord for saying that he was going to die in Jerusalem. Dying young did not fit Peter's agenda, and so he was not receptive to the Lord's plans. Instead, he tried to talk Jesus out of God's plan. That's when Jesus rebuked him.

How often in your prayers do you spend the entire time telling God something? Something you want? Something you don't want? Something you want changed? How often in your prayers do you sit really quietly?

If we could listen, really listen, to our Lord, it would mean putting our talk and interests aside for awhile and paying attention to what God is saying. It is a challenge, but not impossible, to "Listen for the word of the Lord."

Let us pray:
Lord, help me to listen to you today. Make me be silent long enough, and pay attention close enough, to give your word a chance to be heard. And what I have heard, grant me the strength to carry out. In Jesus' name. Amen.

January 29, 1995

READ IN YOUR BIBLE: Matthew 20:17-28
SUGGESTED PSALM: Psalm 146
SUGGESTED HYMNS: Holy God, We Praise Thy Name (E, F, L, P, UM, W)
My Hope Is Built (B, C, F, L, P, UM)

Welcome the Savior

Matthew 20:17-28 contains two distinct stories that seem unrelated at first; however, they can be linked in an odd way. The first, verses 17-19, is Jesus plainly telling his disciples that he is going to suffer and die in Jerusalem, where he is about to enter as King. Naturally, we can presume on the basis of their reactions to Jesus' previous two predictions of his death that this goes against their expectations of what Jesus would do as King.

This lack of understanding links this passage with the story that follows it. In that story, the wife of Zebedee asks Jesus to grant her two sons (both disciples) special status when he is King. Like the disciples, she understandably assumes that kingship mean greatness and power. But to Jesus, greatness and leadership mean giving up power and becoming a humble servant. In each part of Matthew 20:17-28, Jesus is aware that he will give up his life soon.

In the triumphant entry into Jerusalem, the Pharisees hold Jesus responsible for the praise of the crowd, as though they expect him to issue an edict (as a king could) to stop it. Instead, on the way he noticed two blind men and healed them! Like the disciples and the wife of Zebedee, the Pharisees have not yet understood the greatness of service.

* * *

A cartoon depicts a spaceship that has landed on earth. The aliens are shaped like a human arm, with their head region looking like a hand outstretched to shake hands. The man who sees the aliens getting off the spaceship understandably responds to what he sees as an outstretched hand of greeting. He seizes the "hand" and shakes vigorously. Unfortunately, he has actually shaken the alien by the head.

Jesus received various kinds of receptions, beginning with a prophetic rejection at the door of the inn and ending with his rejection by the Jewish and Roman authorities. His most glorious welcome, when he rode into Jerusalem, was based on a misunderstanding that rivals that of the man who shook the alien by the head. The crowd was enthusiastic in their greeting, probably because they thought Jesus would liberate them from the Roman oppressors, in short, because of what they thought he could do for them. They were not enthusiastic about the message, "Whoever wishes to be great among you must be your servant" (Matthew 20:26). The disciples, in spite of all the time they spent listening to Jesus teach, also failed to comprehend the meaning of his entry into Jerusalem. So did the wife of Zebedee.

So what exactly were the disciples supposed to understand? Jesus' verbal answer is found in Matthew 20:26-28, and his answer by example is found in his willingness to enter Jerusalem and go to his death on behalf of many. In other words, he tried to teach us how to humble ourselves and serve others.

There are still plenty of misunderstandings that lead us to welcome Christ but miss his point. When some people give, they often quietly wonder, "What's in it for me?" Any pride in doing for others is a clear sign that our intentions are inappropriate. It is interesting to ponder whether people would still welcome Christ into their lives if there was no such thing as heaven. This question gets to the root of our motivation. Why do we welcome Christ? Is it because we want something out of it, like heaven or prestige, or because we truly believe serving others without reward is the right way to live? The Lord came to show us how to serve, but humanity, thinking it was greeting the message with enthusiasm, instead injured the messenger.

Let us pray:
Lord, when you came into the world that you created, you deserved to be welcomed by the people you came to serve. Instead, you were born in the stable because there was no room in the inn. You spent your adult years wandering—sometimes welcomed, sometimes scorned. Now, as you seek to come into our lives, help us, welcome you with love and devotion. Amen.

February 5, 1995
READ IN YOUR BIBLE: John 6:30-40
SUGGESTED PSALM: Psalm 23
SUGGESTED HYMNS: Let Us Break Bread Together (B, E, F, L, P, UM, W)
Break Thou the Bread of Life (B, C, F, L, P, UM)

Celebrating the Covenant

This conversation about the living bread can be compared to the conversation Jesus had with the woman at the well about the living water (John 4:1-42). The conversation about the living water occurred shortly after people at the wedding in Cana were thirsty, so Jesus changed some water into wine. This conversation about the bread occurs shortly after the miracle of the multiplying bread when the multitude was hungry. In fact, this relationship between act and conversation is repeated in a similar fashion in John (Jesus is the "light of the world," then heals a blind man; Jesus is the "resurrection and the life," then raises Lazarus from the dead).

This conversation about Jesus as the living bread connects nicely to the lesson today in Matthew 26:20-30 (the institution of the Lord's Supper). Living water (changed to wine) and the bread of life satisfy a different longing than ordinary water from a well or bread baked in an oven. When we eat and drink these ordinary gifts, our physical needs are met. But Jesus is saying that just as we regularly need food to meet our physical needs, we also need his continuing presence for the nourishment and life of our soul. Through Communion, Jesus established a way for his disciples to celebrate the "new covenant," his body and blood symbolized by bread and wine. A simple, everyday physical need is tranformed to meet a spiritual need.

* * *

Through the need to translate a letter our church received from Russia, I had the opportunity to get to know a professor from the University of Moscow who was teaching for a year in the United States. As I drove her home from our church (where she had translated the letter to our congregation), she asked whether I could stop by a large grocery store she saw on the way. She wanted to try to find Russian bread.

During the time we spent together that day, she told me about the long food lines in Russia and the staggering prices. As a professor in Russia, her salary at the time had been 3,500 rubles a month. However, she said, if you could find it, butter cost 1,000 rubles. Therefore, many Russians have been living on bread and potatoes.

As we entered the huge grocery store, she said that one of the most impressive things to her about America was the tremendous choice we had in food items, including different brands of the same kind of food, all available to pick up off the shelf and buy without waiting in day-long lines. However, in spite of all the food stocked on the shelves, what she missed most was true Russian bread—a staple in her life until coming to America. In the deli, she sampled several dark rye breads, one of which was even labeled "Russian bread." Naturally, it was too sweet—an American version of the bread she craved.

With her husband still in Russia, I began to wonder whether it was more than just the bread she wanted. After all, why would such a plain commodity mean so very much to her? I suspected that it symbolized to her a person she loved and a culture she missed. She never did find true Russian bread, even in that grocery super-store, and it was easy to sense her disappointment as we left empty-handed.

As Christians, we are like foreigners in a strange land, surrounded by a wide variety of goods when what we really need is a certain kind of bread. The "bread" of money, so valued by our culture, does not satisfy our deepest longings. That is why we approach the altar to receive bread. Along with the wine, we must have this Communion meal to know peace. But it is not just the symbol of this act. Our souls never find peace until we have Christ, the bread of life.

Let us pray:
O Lord, like a loving parent, you provided manna in the desert for the Israelites, and today you provide us with our daily food. We thank you for breaking bread with us just as you did with the disciples so long ago. We find in your daily presence, and in the act of receiving Communion, that you are the bread of life. Help us to feast on your presence and grow stronger in our faith each day. We pray this in Jesus' name. Amen.

February 12, 1995
READ IN YOUR BIBLE: Isaiah 53:1-12
SUGGESTED PSALM: Psalm 128
SUGGESTED HYMNS: O Perfect Love (B, F, L, P, UM)
When I Survey the Wondrous Cross (B, C, E, F, L, P, UM)

Experiencing Rejection

When Christians read Isaiah 53:1-12, they naturally interpret these words in the light of the rejection, suffering, and atoning death of Jesus. In fact, it is startling to realize that Isaiah wrote these words some 700 years before the events recorded in today's lesson, Matthew 26:57-68.

These words originally had a different meaning to Isaiah and his contemporaries. Knowing Isaiah often called the Israelites God's "servant," it is probable that Isaiah used poetic, personal images to describe the sufferings of the Hebrews (these words were written after the Exile, when the Hebrew community was crushed, imprisoned, and scattered throughout Babylonia).

In Jewish thought at that time, suffering was seen as punishment for sins committed. However, once the suffering was ended, it also removed the guilt and prepared one for renewed life. Understood in this way, this passage would have meant that the sufferings of the Israelite people were not only punishment for their sins, but they also prepared the way for this servant to lead other nations to God. Some scholars also suggest that these words might have referred to the sufferings and eventual recognition of King Jehoiachin (see 2 Kings 25:27-30), since those events happened at about the same time this portion of Isaiah (chaps. 40–55) was written.

* * *

One of the more creative marriage proposals I have ever heard was by a young man who took his girlfriend for a ride in a private plane. He flew the plane over a huge garden in which he had planted hundreds of flowers to form the letters of her name, followed by the words, "Please marry me." It is good she said yes, because he would have had a hard time finding someone else to propose to who had the same name.

When we think of proposals, we often think of marriage.

However, we experience or give many proposals in life. We say to our spouse, "Let's go out to eat tonight," and she or he can then reply, "Sure," or "No, let's not." We propose a meeting time to a customer, a raise to our boss, a money-maker for our Sunday school class, a book idea to a publisher, an opportunity to mow the grass to a restless teen. Every time we try to get another person to accept our ideas, our friendship, or our plan of action, we issue a proposal.

It is at these moments that we risk the pain of rejection. After planting and caring for all those flowers, the young suitor in the plane would have faced a bitter flight home if she had said, "Oh, that's a cute idea, but since you took so long to ask I agreed to marry someone else last weekend."

By sending Jesus into the world, God has made a proposal to all of humanity. It is interesting that many comparisons are made between marriage and the relationship between Christ (the bridegroom) and the church (the bride). Those in the church are those who have said yes to God's proposal, and those who are not are those who are still saying no. Isaiah described God's servant as someone who had to undergo painful, humiliating rejection. Matthew, as well as the other Gospels, paints a mournful picture of that rejection. Some people made up lies about Jesus, some spit in his face, some struck him, some mocked him, and some crucified him.

It is ironic that God is the one proposing to us when we need the love of God, our creator, so desperately; we should be proposing the new covenant through Christ instead of the other way around. But God has been good enough to propose a life of love and close relationship to us. It is much better to say yes than to turn away from the beautiful garden God has so lovingly prepared. But that is precisely what we regularly do. Every day God repeats the proposal. And every day we vacillate. Our great goal is to accept the proposal without reservation.

Let us pray:
O Lord, we remember with pain the way your Son, Jesus Christ, was and still is being rejected by so many people. Sometimes that rejection is expressed rudely and sometimes by an apathetic absence. We pray that you would find acceptance in our hearts today and always. Amen.

February 19, 1995

READ IN YOUR BIBLE: John 3:14-21
SUGGESTED PSALM: Psalm 72:12-19
SUGGESTED HYMNS: O Morning Star, How Fair and Bright (E, L, P, UM, W)
Rock of Ages (B, C, E, F, L, UM)

Suffering for Others

The verses of today's devotional reading, John 3:14-21, are part of Jesus' conversation with Nicodemus. They contain one of the most famous verses of the entire Bible. It is difficult to watch a ballgame on television without seeing someone hold up a sign on camera that reads, "John 3:16." While God's unfathomable love for humankind is not the kernel of today's scripture, it is the soil in which the seed grows.

When the content of this verse is isolated from the larger context of John 3:14-21 it does not summarize the point of today's lesson, which is that Jesus must suffer for the sake of others. This suffering is recounted in Matthew 27 as Jesus is tried, sentenced to die, and insulted and abused on the cross.

Another theme linking today's scriptures is belief. In John, Nicodemus's questions were those of someone exploring his beliefs. It is interesting that Matthew would quote the mockings of unbelievers when Jesus hung on the cross. The thrust of their shouts was, "If you save yourself, then I'll believe."

* * *

All animals, including humans, have the instinct for self-preservation. Scientists believe that the apparent exceptions, such as a mother animal risking her life to lead a predator away from a hidden baby, is still seeking the survival of the species; therefore, it is not like thinking, "Well, that predator needs to eat, so I guess I'll let it eat me."

Jesus spoke to Nicodemus and demonstrated in Matthew what it meant for him to be self-giving. This is the conflict for humanity: Our animal nature tells us to save ourselves, while our Lord has shown us how to rise above our animal instincts—love one another, put others first, be self-sacrificial.

When I think of suffering for the sake of others, I think of that welcomed/dreaded phone call, "In late July there is going to be a camp for Jr. High. Will you be a counselor?" What those words mean is "Are you willing to give up a week you could spend doing other things to slap mosquitoes, choke on the superheated Midwest humidity with no air conditioning, and go without sleep while being responsible for sixty children who think they are adults but still tell obnoxious grade-school jokes?" If you say yes, you will indeed sacrifice your time and interests to let somebody else's youth, who don't have enough people in their everyday lives to listen to their jokes, know that they are important people. Yet in the end, you go back to your air-conditioned home knowing that for seven precious days you somehow gained a better understanding of the love of Jesus. Camp counselors who have to ask "What's in it for me?" are usually disappointed with the paycheck!

Those who insulted and abused Jesus on the cross said, "If you are who you say you are, save yourself—then we will believe." They missed the point—Jesus was not trying to save himself. He was giving himself. Yet most of the world is trying to save themselves, like animals do. We work for money to feed and clothe ourselves. We install security devices so we will feel safe. We say nothing that might make us look bad. We give enough to feel less guilty, but deeply treasure our pension accounts so we can live well after retirement. Much of our daily energy is geared toward "saving ourselves."

This is the misleading appeal of John 3:16 considered in isolation—it seems to speak of a way to save ourselves in eternity, too: belief in Jesus. While it is true that believers will have eternal life through Christ, there is much more to belief than simply agreeing that Jesus is the Son of God. As James put it, "Even the demons believe, and tremble in fear." If we truly believe with our lives, then we will live for others in spite of the sacrifice for ourselves. That is not our natural way, but it is Jesus' way.

Let us pray:
O Lord, thank you for showing us the way to give of ourselves. Were it not for your sacrificial giving on our behalf, we would not be able to know the meaning of true other-centered love. We ask you to strengthen us in our times of suffering, and enable us to love one another as you have first loved us. This we pray in your name, amen.

February 26, 1995

READ IN YOUR BIBLE: Acts 10:34-48
SUGGESTED PSALM: Psalm 117
SUGGESTED HYMNS: In Christ There Is No East or West (all)
                Christ Is Made the Sure Foundation (B, E, F, L, P, UM, W)

Follow the Leader

In the early church, Peter (an apostle of Jesus) and Paul (a convert after Jesus' death and resurrection) had a conflict. Peter advocated the idea that anyone who became Christian also had to keep the Jewish laws and customs, even if he or she had not been Jewish before converting to Christianity. Paul, on the other hand, did not think that keeping the Jewish laws was a necessity for Christians. They settled their dispute by dividing the world between the Jewish and Gentile (non-Jewish) parts. Peter preached to Jews, and Paul to Gentiles.

Besides keeping the two strong leaders apart, this arrangement fit their individual ideas. That is why it is astounding to see Peter preaching to Gentiles in Acts 10, and then when they received the gift of the Holy Spirit, advocating their immediate baptism. His message in verses 34-35 is key: "I truly understand that God shows no partiality, but . . . anyone who fears him and does what is right is acceptable to him." This realization lies at the root of Jesus' great commission, "Go therefore and make disciples of all nations" (Matthew 28:19). It paves the way to evangelize all, both Jew and Gentile, and for a new understanding between Peter and Paul.

* * *

Recently I visited a member of our church at his office. He is a salesperson, and as I looked around his office I noticed the tools of his trade. A large map of Illinois adorned the wall, covered with pins with various colored heads. Concentric circles drawn on the map indicated towns within a ten-mile, hundred-mile, and two-hundred-fifty mile drive from his hometown. On a desk nearby was a multi-line telephone, not off in the corner, but right in the center. A large erasable board was mounted on the wall next to his desk, listing numerous potential clients, their phone numbers, and an "x" in various columns next to their names to indicate what stage of business he was in with each one. Another part of the room contained samples of his products, many of them clearly bundled up for his next trip on the road. File folders were arranged on a shelf, and a few key files were placed in a rack—those, he said, were sales he had recently made and people who needed their orders filled. He worked, along with several other salespeople, under the direction of a boss whose job it was to sell as much of the company's product as possible.

I envied his office, wishing that more church offices and Christian homes had rooms geared for reaching out to people. The room reflected a zeal and a deliberate effort to convince people to buy a product they really need. Instead, I think many Christians today are shy about talking about their faith. Somehow they forget that faith is something people need and something they can supply. It is an art to work a conversation to a point where you have the opportunity to share the good news of Jesus Christ with someone, but for many Christians, it is a lost art.

Still, like the salesperson who is under the direction of a boss who wants to increase sales and cover the potential market effectively, Christians are under the leadership of Jesus, who said, "Go, then to all peoples everywhere and make them my disciples." That statement, along with many individuals like Peter discovering that the gospel transcends the cultural box in which they are born, has led to countless missionary ventures. America was discovered, in part, because Christians believed that their message was also for the natives of other lands. One wonders how the world would be different today if Jesus had instead said, "It is better for Christians to mind their own business." Well, Jesus did not say that, so more Christians need to get an erasable board, map the neighborhood, pick up the phone, and learn to share the gospel with anyone who will listen.

Let us pray:
Lord, forgive us for treating your good news as if it were an organizational secret. Remind us that it is a message for people who are different from us as well as for our immediate neighbors. Grant us courage to mention your name out loud, to give you credit for our blessings, and to become a witness for you. In Christ's we pray, amen.

March 5, 1995

READ IN YOUR BIBLE: 1 Corinthians 1:18-25
SUGGESTED PSALM: Psalm 49:1-4, 16-20
SUGGESTED HYMNS: Go to Dark Gethsemane (E, F, L, P, UM)
Were You There (all)

Speaking Spiritual Truth

The Corinthian church was founded amid great luxury and materialism. Corinth was a thriving seaport, rich and populous. At the pinnacle of the city was a great temple built to honor Aphrodite, the Greek Goddess of love. Prostitution was legalized, corruption widespread.

The entire book of 1 Corinthians shows the church's very real struggles to commit to the Way of the Cross in the midst of a secular society. Furthermore, it pictures the struggles within the Christian community as the multitude of problems of the Greek society were repeated within the church.

Paul acknowledges that there are different needs and different problems for members of the church as it seeks to establish and understand itself and its faith. Jews need to have signs; Greeks (Gentiles) must have logic (vv. 22-23). But both these requirements are a hindrance to accepting Jesus the Christ.

With this backdrop, Paul calls upon the church to live without dependence on power or wealth, but merely depending upon the love of Christ as shown in his willingness to die for humankind. This made little sense to the Corinthian world, as Paul acknowledges when he writes, "The message about the cross is foolishness to those who are perishing, but to us who are being saved it is the power of God" (v. 18).

* * *

Of course, this could easily be a letter written to the Christian church today. Our true heritage is the cross. Paul is not speaking simply of the belief that Jesus died and was resurrected. He is telling the church that we must follow Christ's example, thereby doing what is foolishness to the world.

This message goes against the grain of every secular message in today's world: be successful in a career, make money, look attractive, live well, be popular. Like the Corinthians, we are easily seduced by the world, even in the church. Marketing principles have made their way into our churches as we think of ways to make the church attractive: "Come to our new user-friendly 12:45 recovery service." Often we try to make our theology intellectually acceptable or emotionally pleasurable: "Learn why you never had a chance to resist temptation." But we are called by Paul to make the criteria for our decision making, not self-interest, but the shadow of the cross.

Obviously, it's easier said than done. But congregations such as the Church of the Savior in Washington, D.C., have discovered the richness of this call. At the heart of their membership covenant is the pledge to live as servants, finding their call as cross bearers. Imagine the richness in our communities if congregations around the country discovered this call to be their own.

A friend of mine recently struggled with a career choice between directing a highly respected Montessori program for young children and teaching a small class of "special kids," children with multiple handicaps. As she debated between the two, she bounced her feelings and considerations off of her community of faith, asking us to help her discern which was her call. Without hesitation, those of us who know her well encouraged her to work with the "special kids," even though that position was less prestigious and less financially secure. She listened. She chose to work with those children. And she has discovered a tremendous joy and fulfillment in this work, despite its difficulty and the lack of dramatic results.

How do we appropriate this for our lives? Most of us are confused about what is wise for us as Christians; many of us are spiritually immature. Clearly we need Paul to speak spiritual truth to us. And we need, as Christians, to speak spiritual truth to one another in our congregations, calling each other to follow "the foolishness of the cross."

Let us pray:
Loving God, so often we act without thought of you or our calling. So often we are easily misled by the world's alluring temptations. Open our hearts to your will. And teach us the wisdom to discern your workings in our community of faith. In Jesus' name, amen.

March 12, 1995
READ IN YOUR BIBLE: Romans 12:1-10
SUGGESTED PSALM: Psalm 30
SUGGESTED HYMNS: Lord, Whose Love Through Humble Service (E, L, P, UM, W)
Where Cross the Crowded Ways (C, E, F, L, P, UM)

Faithfulness in Difficult Times

When Paul writes these words to the Christian church in Rome, he is giving concrete instructions about living in Christian community, not just advice about individual behavior. In the first verse he redefines worship as much more than a gathering of believers; it is the offering of ourselves to God as a "living sacrifices." They were "not to be conformed to the world" (v. 2).

Paul refuses to back off or dilute the gospel. In discerning the will of God he fully expected the church to find itself out of step with the world. This is a tremendously big assignment. Live in the world, but not be conformed? But Paul does not demand the impossible. He gives practical advice, reminding them that they are a community and have many talents (vv. 4-8). What they cannot accomplish individually, they can do collegially.

* * *

The word *sacrifice* probably made the early church as uncomfortable as it does us. After all, Paul urged them to be utterly transformed. This letter could so easily have been written to the twentieth-century church! How tempting it is for today's church to water down Paul's words to make them palatable. If as a community of faith we accept this Christian transformation, we might stop worrying about raising a large budget or building more impressive buildings. We might minister to those outside the gathered community—the hungry, the poor, prisoners.

To be a transformed people, a living sacrifice, is a serious call. It requires all of our commitment, not just part of it. In today's church the words may sound outdated, even unhealthy. Aren't we tempted to label his words "ideals" that are at once unrealistic and impossible, though admirable?

But for Paul the words were not ideals but realities. He had given up everything—his prestigious position as a Pharisee, his wealth, his reputation—to preach a radical message of discipleship. Transformation for Paul meant an altogether new life in Jesus Christ.

Years ago, doing peace work in West Tennessee, my husband and I met a man whose life exemplified such transformation. Born the son of poverty-stricken farmers, he called himself a converted redneck. He never received more than an eighth-grade education because he had to go to work to support himself. When he was asked to be a Sunday school teacher, his life changed. He laughingly admitted that he was convicted by the Sunday school materials! And convicted he was. He began giving away everything he did not need—his extra coats and shoes, books he had read, his savings. He quietly supported young people through college, determined that others would receive the education he was denied. He began to go to church meetings and to quote the gospel. In fact, he became a thorn in the side of institutional church leaders because he kept insisting that not just individual Christians but the church was called to follow the example of Jesus Christ. Until his death in 1991, he insisted that the church be racially inclusive and be involved directly with the poor. And even in his eighties he could be found in the nursing homes, visiting with the elderly, paying their bills, even buying them shoes and tending to their most basic needs—all for the love of Christ.

The Christian church today is called to this transformed life in Christ. More than likely we will find ourselves out of step with our culture as we turn our lives over to Christ. We might, for example, live on what we need, not what we want, realizing that our life-style affects people in need all over the world. We might sacrifice our good name, our professional position, or even our religious standing in order to live as Christians in this world. But this is our freedom, and this is our call.

Let us pray:
Loving God, it is so difficult to follow you! You call us to transformed lives, and we want to cling to our old ways. You promise us new life, and we hold fast to death. Help us realize that as we follow you and allow ourselves to become "living sacrifices," you will bring us joy beyond measure. Amen.

March 19, 1995

READ IN YOUR BIBLE: Ephesians 6:10-18
SUGGESTED PSALM: Psalm 64
SUGGESTED HYMNS: I Love Thy Kingdom, Lord (B, C, E, F, L, UM)
Come Down, O Love Divine (E, L, P, UM, W)

Resisting Temptation

A cosmic battle is taking place, according to Paul, a battle against superhuman forces of evil. Paul was writing from prison, and he may have been writing to himself as much as to the church in order to keep faith during that difficult time. He was certainly expecting persecution, for he describes God's armor in order to fortify the Christian to stand his or her ground when circumstances are at their worst.

Paul begs the church to be in prayer in the Spirit on every occasion (v. 18). The Spirit is the one Jesus promised to send to comfort and aid the people. Now Paul is claiming this comfort and aid. This exhortation clearly demonstrates Paul's understanding of the dangers of the times and the special needs of the church.

But Paul is also certain of the help God provides through this armor. Thus he details it: truth, righteousness, the gospel of peace, faith, salvation, the Word of God (vv. 14-17). What is the Word of God or of salvation but that Christ has walked this road before him and is with him on his journey? Paul believes it so fervently that he stakes his life on it.

* * *

According to theologian Walter Wink, "The powers are not demonic beings floating in the sky; they are rather the corporations, the nation-states, the economic systems and the religious hierarchies that organize and to a great extent dictate the life of human societies."

Although modern days see unprecedented violence and pain, Paul's words about cosmic evil may sound overdramatic. We may imagine that we are in control of those forces today. But it has been only a few years since an American president equated the Soviet government with the forces of evil. With the collapse of Eastern Europe and the Communist bloc, the Western church could easily assume (along with its governments) that evil is at bay.

In any age, Christians must see beneath political events to the ongoing cosmic and spiritual battles. The fall of the communist bloc, for example, has brought with it violent conflicts between various ethnic groups. And racism, addiction, and the breakdown of the family are frequent marks of our society.

In the midst of this spiritual conflict Paul boldly preaches the liberating word of Christ. He knew that the church in any age would always be coming face to face with evil. Therefore he reminds his disciples to be prepared daily by putting on the armor of God. He also insists that they "pray in the Spirit at all times in every prayer and supplication" (verse 18). Wink elaborates on this when he says, "God's hands are effectively tied when we fail to pray. That is the dignity and urgency of our praying.

> History belongs to the intercessors who believe a new way into being . . . we are commissioned to pray for miracles because nothing less is sufficient. We pray to God not because we understand these mysteries but because we have learned from our tradition and from experience that God indeed is sufficient for us, whatever the Powers may do. (Walter Wink, *Engaging the Powers*)

A saint in my church—who would never recognize himself as such—spends every morning in prayer, putting on this armor. There are tangible differences about him—a gentleness, a peace, a deep faith, no matter what the circumstances. He knows that God's armor will sustain him throughout the day, enabling him to resist temptation and empowering him to speak and act boldly for his Lord. While most of us in the church are adrift in addictions we keep carefully hidden, or bewildered in the face of society's pressures, or fearful at the possibility of suffering, this man knows who he is and whose he is. Everyone around him is touched by his witness.

Let us pray:
Loving God, open our eyes to the power of evil in this world. Open our hearts to our complicity in it. Change us, we pray, that we may stand fast in every situation, clutching your armor of love, peace, and forgiveness. And please stand with us, dear Savior, so that we will not be afraid. Amen.

March 26, 1995

READ IN YOUR BIBLE: Colossians 3:8-17
SUGGESTED PSALM: Psalm 67
SUGGESTED HYMNS: Love Divine, All Loves Excelling (all)
   Come, We That Love the Lord (B, C, E, F, UM, W)

Dealing with Differences

Certain themes are woven through Paul's letters to the different churches throughout the Mediterannean area, marking the way in which these churches are similar. The church in Colossae was threatened by a heresy that attacked the supremacy of Christ. False teachers in Colossae were insisting that Christ was not enough to defeat the powers of evil, that certain rituals and laws and philosophies must supplement Christianity to make it more powerful as a religion. Paul reminds the church of the new nature of Christ's community. He asserts that all barriers have been torn down when he proclaims, "There is no longer Greek and Jew, circumcised and uncircumcised, barbarian, Scythian, slave and free, but Christ is all and in all" (v. 11).

According to biblical scholar William Barclay, this verse illustrates the very barriers that Christ has demolished. Greek and Jew, two cultures that despised each other, were eating at table together. Tradition and ritualistic barriers, symbolized by circumcision, were eliminated in the family of God. The Scythian was considered a barbarian, while the Greek was perceived as an aristocrat, so those walls of culture were torn down by the church. Even barriers of class were no longer important as the slave and the free were united in Christ.

How does this miracle occur? To Paul it is simply the work of the living Christ. Throughout Colossians he repeats, "The secret is Christ"; "The secret is this: Christ in you."

* * *

Today, conflicts and divisions abound in our families and communities. Racial, class, sexual, and political differences threaten to tear us apart, even in the church. And we in the church are often afraid to deal with these conflicts; sometimes we even fail to recognize divisions in our communities of faith.

I am continually amazed and disturbed by observing individuals or groups that have many common interests or similarities but choose to focus on their few differences. I am delighted when I discover an exception.

My former church used to have council meetings that often ended in anger and resentment. On these occasions no one felt like he or she had been heard. In desperation our pastor began one tense session with Bible study. Then we prayed. We did not rush into our "business." We focused on Christ rather than on ourselves. And the meeting was transformed. The cross was in our midst. The risen Christ was delivering us, on this occasion, from ourselves.

One year ago this very congregation voted to close its seventy-nine years of proud history. But the vote did not signal giving up on ministry and abandonment of the inner-city. Instead it was a vote to help begin a new interracial church serving the city.

Another church—an African-American congregation—took the same step. When the new church was formed it was not a white church welcoming black members or a black church welcoming white members. It was and is a sign of God establishing a new community, mending the torn cloth of our culture's divisive ways. Paul's words "There is neither Jew nor Greek" have special, very joyful meaning for this congregation. Again and again we say, "This is the work of Christ. We couldn't—wouldn't have done it on our own."

"Let the peace of Christ rule in your hearts: to which indeed you were called in the one body," Paul writes. How difficult it is for us to remember that our community of faith is grounded in and dependent on Christ. Compassion, kindness, humility, genleness, patience—these are Christ's garments, not our abilities. In the midst of serious divisions, Paul's prescription for the church is not a list of virtues but an invitation to receive a gift—the Spirit of the living Christ.

Let us pray:
Gracious God, you have offered us a tremendous gift. You have offered us the Spirit of Christ, which will clothe us with patience, love, compassion, and humility. Open our hearts to accept your gift so that we may be a loving, reconciling presence in your world. Amen.

April 2, 1995

READ IN YOUR BIBLE: Ephesians 4:4-16
SUGGESTED PSALM: Psalm 133
SUGGESTED HYMNS: The Church of Christ, in Every Age (B, L, P, UM, W)
                    Onward, Christian Soldiers (B, C, E, F, L, UM)

Building Up the Body

According to biblical scholar William Barclay, this book introduces the metaphor of the church as the body of Christ. Just as Christ is God's instrument of reconciliation, so also the church is Christ's instrument of reconciliation. The church is the incarnation of Christ in the world, the hands and feet of Christ. This was central to Paul's faith. Because of the importance of this theme to Paul, Barclay believes that he circulated this letter to all the eastern churches to inform them of their task of reconciling the world to God.

In Ephesians 4:4-16 Paul is determined to communicate the oneness of the Body of Christ. "There is one body and one Spirit, just as you were called to the one hope of your calling, one Lord, one faith, one baptism, one God and Father of all, who is above all and through all and in all" (vv. 4-6), he says. And the gifts given by God exist to build up the body of Christ. As part of God's community, Christ's body, we are to use these gifts, no matter how small, to bear witness to a fractured world.

According to Paul, we will reach maturity as Christians when we are unified in our faith. No longer will we be as children, vulnerable to disension and false teachings, unsure of our faith. Indeed, Paul calls the church to "grow up into Christ." Part of growing up is claiming our gift and using it to build up the community.

* * *

As a child, I remember my father, a college administrator, telling me that the people most important to any profession are the janitors who take care of the space of the professionals. He believed that a good relationship with them would enable him to do his job well. Later as a school teacher, I discovered the wisdom of his words. On the first day of school I walked into an empty classroom: no chairs, no desks, no chalkboards. I was totally helpless without the assistance of the janitor. I think about this now as I study Paul's words on gifts. Surely, we seldom, if ever, think about the gift of janitoring. But that first day in the classroom it was a wonderful gift to me

Each of us needs the gifts of others. This is especially true in the community of faith whose task is to bear witness to reconciliation. Many of us discount the gifts of others when we do not also have those same gifts. In my own church there is often tension between the "idea" people and the "detail" people. Those with the grand ideas often do not have a facility for getting the job accomplished. And those who are highly skilled planning the course of action most likely would never have had the dream to fulfill. Neither of us could get much done without the other.

Paul's choice of the body as a metaphor for the church is brilliant—and the more we learn about the body, the more we can appreciate the significance of this image. Every single cell in our bodies must do its job or there is dysfunction and revolt. One of the names for revolt is cancer. Cancer happens when cells decide that they want to govern themselves and change what is in their nature to do. The result is medical chaos and often the death of the entire body. Paul understood body dysfunction.

Many of the churches to whom Paul wrote were divided over the issue of gifts. In Ephesians he reminds them that Christ descended to earth, taking human form, humbling himself in identifying with us. For the body of Christ it is clear: No gift is too small; each is God-given, and all are vital to the working of the Body.

Jesus and Paul both would have understood the gift of janitoring. Jesus was a common carpenter. Paul was a common tentmaker. But they did understand the gifts of the church—large and small.

Let us Pray:
Gracious God, you have called us to be one in the Spirit. You have given each of us a unique gift and place within the Body of Christ. Give us the grace to acknowledge our gift, the courage to use it for your glory, and the love that will unify us in Christ. Amen.

April 9, 1995

READ IN YOUR BIBLE: Psalm 95:1-7
SUGGESTED PSALM: Same
SUGGESTED HYMNS: My Hope Is Built on Nothing Less (B, C, F, L, P, UM)
Let All the World in Every Corner Sing (B, C, E, P, UM, W)

Growing Through Worship

This psalm is a hymn praising God, one that was probably used in ancient worship as a processional. It begins by gathering the community together with "Come!" A great throng of people would be waiting outside the Temple. And as they joined in the singing of this psalm calling them to worship, the priests would blow their trumpets. The procession into the Temple would begin.

This hymn of praise begins with the naming of our God. Most significantly, God is King above all kings. Then God is hailed as the Rock of our salvation. The Old Testament tradition had many references to the rock: the rock that gave the Israelites water in the desert (Exodus 17:1-7), the rock on which the Temple was built (2 Samuel). God as Creator has fashioned the earth. But it is also God as Shepherd who gathers his flock together. As God is named in this psalm, we realize that God is magnificent but God is also personal. God is mighty, and God is also accessible to us humans. God reigns in grandeur, but God also loves His creation with passion.

These verses describe the movements of real worship. We are to worship with joyful songs that tell the story of our deliverance by God. We are to "throw ourselves at God's feet in homage," kneeling before our God in humility. We are to listen to God through the scriptures.

* * *

According to Ted Jennings, in his book *Life as Worship: Prayer and Praise in Jesus' Name*, praise should be a way of life for us. A life-style shaped by praise defies anxiety and bondage to this world's demands; it claims assurance that God loves us and will provide for us. Praise in that sense is revolutionary. It dethrones the powers and principalities by insisting that God is over all things and is in control.

In *Cry Pain, Cry Hope*, Elizabeth O'Connor goes one step further. She writes, "One can learn to think and praise God not only for the good things in life—the joys and delights and blessings—but one can and should also praise God for pain and difficulty, for problems and adversity, for dark and destructive things in our lives . . . we should praise God for the pain and the problems." She adds, "As I conscientiously praised God for what was hard to bear in my life, I discovered that praise for the good became spontaneous. I could not hold it back . . . I was no longer so sure I knew what was good and what was bad."

Some of us are reluctant to be bold in praising God. We don't like to be very expressive or emotional, especially in worship. We like to worship with our heads, not our hearts. In this, we are treating worship as an entertainment rather than an activity. It is something we watch or listen to rather than something we do. Worship, however, can only happen for us when we participate—never when we sit as observers.

But let's be clear: Whenever we celebrate the greatness of God, we are also calling upon God to be God. The same active participation we often avoid in worship, we demand of God. We are calling on God to do the things that he has promised—to bring justice to earth, to lead his people, and to empower us for further participation. We would be wise to consider that if God is active in our lives, our lives will probably be turned upside down! I recently heard of a church that has a novel sign above the door as you exit the sanctuary. The sign says "Disciples Entrance."

Worship, then, is much more than a ritual that brings order and predictability to our Sunday mornings. It is certainly more than an emotional release. It is an act that calls to God and to us to transform the world together. It begins with the gathering of believers on Sunday mornings and extends from there into the world. We must not expect anything less.

Let us pray:
Thank you, Lord, for being our God, for loving us with passion, for creating a glorious world for us, and for blessings beyond number. We praise you not only for what you have done but for what you are going to do. We call upon you to fulfill your promises to us, that your Kingdom may come on earth. Amen.

April 16, 1995

READ IN YOUR BIBLE: Phil. 2:1-11
SUGGESTED PSALM: Psalm 138
SUGGESTED HYMNS: What Wondrous Love Is This (B, E, F, L, P, UM, U)
Fairest Lord Jesus (B, C, E, F, P, UM)

Becoming a Resurrection People

Paul loved the church at Phillipi. It was the first church he founded in Europe. It was also the only church that he allowed to financially support his ministry. Although Paul is writing this letter from prison, his tone throughout is bouyant. "I thank my God every time I remember you, constantly praying with joy in every one of my prayers for all of you," he writes (1:3-4). And in chapter 4, his letter overflows with love for them as he says, "Therefore, brothers and sisters, whom I love and long for, my joy and crown, stand firm in the Lord in this way" (4:1).

Paul begins chapter 2 encouraging the healthy community spirit at Philippi: loving consolation, warmth of affection, and a common care for unity. Then he quotes an ancient Christian hymn that sees Christ as the embodiment of humility in his willingness to forego his lordship, become human and accept the agonizing death on a cross. He emphasizes Christ's downward mobility by pointing out that Jesus has: 1. made himself nothing; 2. assumed the nature of a slave; 3. taken on human shape; 4. humbled himself; 5. accepted the degradation of death on a cross. By quoting this hymn, Paul wants to make it clear that there is nothing we are called to that Christ hasn't experienced first. Christ goes before us on the road to servanthood; Christ goes before us into death. And—joy of all joys—Christ goes before us into life everlasting.

* * *

When I visited Nicaragua years ago during that country's civil war, my delegation had the opportunity to meet with mothers who had lost their sons in the fighting. One by one, eyes brimming with tears, they told us of the deaths of their beloved sons in a war they had not chosen and could not support. It became utterly clear to me that to them resurrection was not an ideal; it was a fact. And they were absolutely certain, that Jesus was walking their path of pain with them.

When we asked them why they did not despair, they replied, "We cannot despair when Christ is by our side." They understood what Paul was describing. They took Christ's journey through life and death as seriously as their own, never doubting that he embraced suffering, poverty, and death in order to identify with them. It was startling that such intense sorrow could be possible without despair and loss of faith. I found myself envious of their calm certainty as I realized that I have been too insulated from suffering and death to understand what it means to have Christ accompany me as he was accompanying those Nicaraguan mothers.

We as the church will become resurrection people when we face death. And let's not kid ourselves. We will face death. Physical death, disillusionment, poverty, divorce—all of these are deaths, ones we try to avoid and most often try to deny. But for the Christian community these are points of contact with the Lord, who loves us so fiercely that he has defeated death, every expression of death that threatens us.

This victory over the sorrows of life is not through elimination of the sorrows. They remain. But their continuing presence is not experienced as something imposed upon us by an uncaring God and an inadequate Savior. The continuing presence of pain and suffering is shared entirely by our God and Savior. And for those persons who experience this sense of shared living, the question of "why" is invalidated. It no longer matters.

For Paul, for the church at Philippi, for mothers who have lost their sons in Nicaragua, and for us (no matter our sorrow), this is the basis of joy. We are not alone. Our Father, the Son, and the Holy Spirit are with us. In our suffering, there is healing; in our death, there is resurrection. In all things we can rejoice.

Let us pray:
Gracious God, sometimes it is so difficult to see resurrection. We feel utterly lost in death and despair. Give us eyes to see the life around us and to celebrate the victory that Christ has won for us. In Christ's name, amen.

April 23, 1995

READ IN YOUR BIBLE: Romans 15:1-13
SUGGESTED PSALM: Psalm 148
SUGGESTED HYMNS: Lift Every Voice and Sing (B, E, L, P, UM, W)
O Come, All Ye Faithful (all)

Exercising Christian Freedom

In Romans 14 Paul addresses the issue of eating or refusing certain foods, contending that foods in themselves are neither clean nor unclean. He walks the fine line between legalism—which states that Christians should abstain from certain foods—and permissiveness by begging the community, "Do not, for the sake of food, destroy the work of God" (14:20).

So in chapter 15, he continues this discussion by urging the community of faith to notice the weaker ones in the fellowship and to act to build up their faith. In other words, he is defining freedom within the loving community as the willingness to let our actions be dictated by the needs of others, putting ourselves second to the building up of the common life.

Paul clearly believes that Jesus' way of life cannot be lived in isolation. Individuals must live in community (15:2). And the community must move beyond its homogeneous parochialism to include others with different customs (15:9). Paul says to welcome one another. Welcoming someone is more than accepting someone. It offers hospitality. It projects joyfulness. And all of this is for the purpose of "glorifying the God and Father of our Lord Jesus Christ" (15:6).

* * *

Today, it may be appropriate to give Paul's words a larger interpretation. Common life is no longer simply our individual relationships within the local church, but common life now extends throughout the world. In this context building up the common life might mean that we take into account the global community when making choices.

Thus we would make life-style choices carefully, realizing our connectedness with nature and with people in other countries. We would stop squandering natural resources as though they were unlimited; we would not buy from companies that exploit workers; we would stop investing in businesses that build weapons; we might even set aside our own weapons and live by the law of love.

Living by the law of love means accepting and appreciating another's customs, having compassion for those who have insufficient nutrition and sharing the wealth, believing in the possibility that others may know a better way to accomplish something than we do, and leading rather than pushing.

We are not accustomed to having our freedoms curtailed for any reason, least of all the common good. It sounds frightening—even anti-democratic. Paul wasn't debating politics, however, he was simply pointing out that the Christian has much more to consider than his or her own welfare.

But let's be clear: this is not paternalistic, nor does it have an ulterior motive. It is seeing choices from a longer perspective, a wider perspective than we normally see them, trusting that our actions are significant in helping to fulfill God's Kingdom on earth.

A friend of mine has five children but has chosen to live on a minimal salary. She does not have air-conditioning for her home; she buys from a food co-op rather than from a mega grocery store; and she and her children walk or ride bikes rather than drive everywhere they need to go. She has simply decided that her choices have long-term consequences and that she is going to be less comfortable now so that her children's children might have more resources available to them. It sounds ridiculous that someone would take so seriously what might happen years from now. But I suspect that she is taking her Christian freedom and witness very seriously.

It is true that whether or not we eat certain foods is not the issue. It is also true that every single choice we make contributes to or detracts from the common good. What power we have—and what responsibility!

Let us pray:
Loving God, each of us has a different understanding of what Christian freedom means. Broaden our vision, Lord, so that we realize how much our actions affect others, not only nearby but worldwide. Let us act in faith so that the way we live does make a difference. In Jesus' name, amen.

April 30, 1995

READ IN YOUR BIBLE: Galatians 6:1-10
SUGGESTED PSALM: Psalm 32
SUGGESTED HYMNS: For the Beauty of the Earth (all)
Lord, I Want to Be a Christian (B, C, F, P, UM)

Sharing One Another's Pain

Galatians 6 begins with Paul making a distinction between those who intentionally sow evil, choosing their "lower" natures, and those who slip and make mistakes. Earlier in Galations, he has graphically detailed the path of evil (5:19-21), warning that "Those who do such things will not inherit the kingdom of God." Here, his tone changes, as he recommends that the Christian community recognize the difference between intentionally sowing evil and doing wrong on impulse. Rather than being legalistic, the community must reach out in love and gentleness to those who slip into sin.

Paul, practicing the gentleness he recommends for others, points out that those who feel themselves righteous and capable of judging other, are mistaken (6:3). Temptation comes to all, and resistance can be hard. It is not enough to resist temptation. It is necessary to bear one another's burden of sin and to help one another resist (6:10).

* * *

Surely we all know how difficult it is to gently set a brother or sister right again (6:1). Judging them or remaining silent is the easier and more comfortable course to take.

When a member of our church community was slipping off of his Twelve-Step program, several of us noticed, but for a long time remained silent. When an eighteen-year-old became pregnant outside of wedlock, we knew she needed us more than ever to help her chart a more redemptive course for her life. But at first it was easier to shake our heads, throw up our hands, and judge her for her mistake.

In both of these situations we eventually acted. Members of the church intervened with the friend who was drinking. They acted in love, not judgment. We all remembered the time that our brother who was slipping had reached out to a street alcoholic who had wandered into our Sunday morning worship. After doing what he could to help the man, he had wept, "There but for the grace of God go I." It was very difficult for us to intervene with our friend. But he needed help, and grace meant firmly but gently insisting that he return to treatment.

With the pregnant young woman, it was even more difficult. She was so inclined to hear judgment rather than love. Nonetheless, we gathered together to talk her through her choices and to let her know we were not going to abandon her.

As we share each other's burdens, a miracle occurs. We have a greater understanding of each other and are less inclined to judge. We realize that we are all struggling to be faithful, and that we are all dealing with problems. Paul puts it, "For everyone has his own proper burden to bear."

In an urban church near us, neighborhood youth, almost without warning, began attending the church's Wednesday night suppers. The congregation was all white and mostly elderly, while the youth were mostly black and quite energetic! Many of the church people were scared and felt threatened. One even suggested closing down their midweek fellowship! But the pastor and a member who was ready to work with the youth insisted that this was an opportunity for all to grow together. The youth, tempted by violence and the drug culture, needed the church community. The church community, dying rapidly because of its fear of change, needed the youth. Fears and all, they are all working at it. They are learning to share one another's burdens.

Maybe that is why Paul is so insistent that we bear one another's burdens. Like the old fable about the tree of troubles, whenever given the opportunity to choose trouble other than the one we bear, we usually choose our own! We realize that, given someone else's circumstances, we might act as he or she does. We realize, "there but for the grace of God go I."

Let us pray:

Lord, at times we all need comfort and encouragement, especially when our burdens become too heavy to bear alone. Let us remember to share our burdens with others as well as to be there for others to lighten their load. In Christ's name, amen.

May 7, 1995

READ IN YOUR BIBLE: Galations 5:13-26
SUGGESTED PSALM: Psalm 1
SUGGESTED HYMNS: Love Divine, All Loves Excelling (all)
O God of Love, O God of Peace (B, E, L, P, W)

Committed to Serve

For some early believers it was tempting to see the freedom of the gospel as a freedom to do anything, believing in God's ultimate forgiveness. But in Galations Paul reminds the community that Christian freedom is the freedom to love responsibly. He warns that without such love the church community will be filled with anger and resentment and will ultimately fail.

So in verses 19-21 Paul lists the desires of the lower nature. Notice that they sound frantic, out of control, and divisive of community. In contrast, Paul talks about the "fruits" of the Spirit. Fruits are the outcome of good gardening. By tending to our spiritual lives, we produce a harvest of desirable attributes. By using the image of fruit he conveys the health of these qualities and their positive impact on the believer and the community.

Of course, for Paul, the production of this fruit is not a matter of willpower; it is a matter of turning the old self over to the Lordship of Jesus. The old self is crucified with Christ. And those living in the Spirit are transformed into new creatures. Without grace there is no transformation.

* * *

Centuries later, we are still struggling with our "lower natures"—both individually and corporately. We are often consumed by selfish desires and addictions. Those of us in the church are often torn apart by divisions that seem irreconcilable. As in the church in Galatia, they prevent us from being a community of love.

What then? Honest recognition and confession of our "shadow" side must be the first step. In isolation, we can hide. In the community of the church, we must face ourselves. And let's not fool ourselves! Leaving behind our old selves, our skewered perceptions, our idolatries, our addictions is agonizing. Crucifixion names it well. It is a painful wrenching of ourselves toward health and wholeness, which hurts more than it helps at first.

The community must be involved. It nudges us toward health, either by insisting on a recovery program or by helping us find someone to talk to or by calling us to accountability. And it is necessary for us to listen to the advice of our community, to trust in its collective wisdom, to believe in its love and good will for us, and to follow its leading.

But that's not all. The community must teach us to love each other. As Paul puts it, "Be servants to one another in love." Often these lessons come when we least expect them. One Sunday I went to church angry and resentful. It had been a terrible morning trying to get the children ready for church, struggling with getting myself ready, feeding everyone, refereeing their fights. I had arrived at Sunday school quite bedraggled, only to find my children not only fighting with each other but also arguing with their Sunday school teacher! Amid this, a young woman walked up to me to hug me and say hello. I growled at her, too tired and angry to respond to her embrace. She was very hurt, and I was even angrier at myself for being so petty.

During community prayer time at the service, this woman prayed for me. I found myself suddenly aware not only of the power of her love but of my need for it. She had many problems of her own, including where to get her next meal, and she was lifting up my bad mood for healing by God.

"The harvest of the Spirit is love, joy, peace, kindness, goodness, fidelity, gentleness and self-control," writes Paul. We need the community of faith to weed our natures and to help us harvest the crops of the Spirit. And we need God's grace to bind us all together in love.

Let us pray:
Gracious God, so often we are lost in pain, confusion, addictions, and anger. We feel alone, and we turn from you. Please don't give up on us! Forgive us, we pray. Nudge us to wholeness through our communities of faith. Help us to embrace healing so that we may more ably serve you. In Jesus' name, amen.

May 14, 1995

READ IN YOUR BIBLE: 1 John 4:7-21
SUGGESTED PSALM: Psalm 36:5-12
SUGGESTED HYMNS: O Love That Wilt Not Let Me Go (B, C, F, L, P, UM)
　　　　　　　　　Praise to the Lord, the Almighty (B, E, F, L, P, UM, W)

Motivated by Christ's Love

The Christian church to whom this was written was divided. The people claimed to know God (2:3-4), to love God (4:20), and to have close communion with God (1:6). But some of these, the author warns, were false prophets who kept the Body of Christ divided.

The early church was vulnerable to claims by false prophets because, while it believed Jesus was returning soon, it had been waiting a long time. When someone came along promising a quick fix or claiming to be the Christ, it must have thrown the community into confusion. How were they to know the truth?

In 1 John 4 the author, therefore, warns the church to "test the Spirits" and to trust those who acknowledge the reality of the Incarnation. After all, the evidence of God's love for us is the Incarnation of his Son and the willingness of his Son to die for our sins. But the Incarnation doesn't stop there. Because of Christ's sacrifice we are "bound" to love one another. God is also incarnate in us through our love. And the author promises that the love of God filling the community of faith will actually banish any fear that keeps the community divided.

* * *

Surely, the church today can find in this passage a message about our common life. We all know how central love is to the gospel and yet—we are not always bound together in love within the church. We cannot manufacture this love of our free will. It is inextricably tied up with our love for—and our being loved by—Jesus Christ. When God dwells in us we are without fear and we are able to love our brother or sister in Christ. In Luke 10:29-37 Jesus illustrates the extent of what is possible and what is required in loving. This is the story of the good Samaritan.

Years ago I belonged to an "intentional" Christian community. Everything we did focused on following the way of Christ. We were very active in social justice issues and very committed to simplying life-styles. But the community was riddled with fear: fear that someone was judging our work; fear that all our efforts would have negligible results; fear that we were not doing enough to win our salvation or take others to salvation.

As time went on it became more and more difficult to love each other. It became like a bad marriage with patterns that are hard to break. In the name of Christ—whom we professed to love—we tore each other up. And the reason we caused each other so much pain was not bad intentions or the desire to hurt each other; it was fear that something was wrong with us and that we were ultimately unloveable. From the very begiining of our community we had cast our outcome in failure because we had not accepted into our lives the grace that God gave us to succeed.

In contrast, this past year in our city, divided by racial hatred and fear, an interracial church has been founded to witness to a new way of loving. This congregation, aware that 11:00 Sunday morning is the most segregated hour, were determined to incarnate Christ's love by worshiping with their Christian brothers and sisters of a different race. People have come from all over the city to see for themselves that it is possible to gather together—black and white—and to blend different worship traditions into a beautiful new liturgy which over time will become a tradition. The love generated by worshiping together has banished the fear that often separates us from each other.

When we recognize Christ in each other, that our very tarnished love is cleaned and brightened so that once again it shines on everyone around us. We recognize the worth and value of all people and become eager to help others. In short, we become instruments of reconciliation.

Let us pray:
Gracious God, you have called us to work for reconciliation, yet we often stop short because we are afraid. We are afraid that we are unloveable and that we cannot love the way you would have us love. Help us, we pray. In the name of Christ, amen

May 21, 1995
READ IN YOUR BIBLE: Matthew 25:31-41
SUGGESTED PSALM: Psalm 27
SUGGESTED HYMNS: My Shepherd Will Supply My Need (B, E, F, P, W)
  Jesus Calls Us O'er the Tumult (B, C, E, F, L, UM)

Ministry Through Giving

Jesus' final sermon in Matthew ends with the words, "Just as you did it to one of the least of these. . . ." Earlier in chapter 25 he has told the parable of the bridesmaids. There he seems to be warning his disciples that, though the return of the bridegroom will be joyous, it will be delayed. And the church must be ready for the delay. We must have enough oil in our lamps for the long night of waiting.

That story is followed by the familiar parable of the talents. Again, it is a long time before the master returns to settle accounts with his servants. The servants who took the risk of investing their talents are rewarded. The one who is fearful and reluctant to use what he'd been given ends up losing what little he had.

These two stories are the backdrop for Jesus' finale in Matthew, the story of the last judgment. The ultimate criterion for being "righteous" (manifesting God's grace) is service. Not doctrine, not theology, not proper church attire, not even church attendance, but acts of hospitality toward the least of those in the Kingdom. The church must be in loving relationship with those who are in need. That is how it will best serve the risen Lord.

Following the sermon in Matthew 25, Jesus tells his disciples that he will be delivered up to be crucified. The apex of giving is sacrificing one's life. The church, in following Christ, must be prepared for a long wait, must be willing to risk, must serve the least of those in the Kingdom, and finally, must be willing to follow Christ to the cross.

* * *

The church of today has made the works listed in chapter 25 harder and harder to perform by being set apart from the very suffering it is called to address. How many of us are really in touch with those who are hungry or naked or imprisoned? How many of us welcome the stranger into our homes or go into the prisons? We gloss over these words or apply them to people within our fellowship. But Jesus is describing a community of faith that knows the poor, the outcast, the homeless, the imprisoned—knows names and faces and stories. Of course, this requires a church in the neighborhoods and on the streets.

Christian singer Ken Medema sings a story of those who build fortress walls and have celebrations that exclude the poor. Meanwhile, unknown to them, the "prince" nightly puts on beggar's clothing and walks the streets below the fortress, loving and healing the forgotten ones. God's community is in the streets.

Clearly, Jesus is not describing a program or a project. He is portraying relationships, which are healing. It is easy for us to dismiss this as "too little, too late" or ineffective strategy. But Jesus never took the easy route. He did not wave his arms and heal the crowd en masse. He touched each person, one by one. I have heard about a pastor who is sometimes criticized for taking the time to get to know one person at a time. He believes that ministry to one person is as important as any program the church can create. He believes in a hospitality in which everyone is known by name.

Finally, notice that Matthew 25 says nothing about results. It doesn't say, for instance, that when the righteous visited those in prison the prisoners never committed another crime. Nor does it imply that once the hungry were fed they never returned for more food. Do you feel the need to solve the world's hunger problem? Do you believe that your personal inability to bring peace to all the world means you are foolish to try? At times we may be called to do what looks utterly ridiculous over and over again! We are not responsible for dramatic results, just for being a neighbor to those in need.

Let us pray:
Gracious and loving God, teach us to be servants to all your people—the homeless, the hungry, the hurting, the imprisoned. Teach us to listen to their stories and to know their names. And help us to see the Christ who lives in all people. Amen.

MAY 28, 1995

READ IN YOUR BIBLE: John 15:9-17
SUGGESTED PSALM: Psalm 111
SUGGESTED HYMNS: Jesus Calls Us O'er the Tumult (B, C, E, F, L, UM)
    Lord, Whose Love Through Humble Service (E, L, P, UM, W)

Serving with Love

Jesus speaks these verses in his final discourse recorded in John—at the Last Supper after Judas has left to betray him. Jesus is addressing his disciples, preparing himself and them for his death. The commandment for them to love one another is repeated throughout this final lesson, as though he is frantic for them to get the message before he is gone from them.

By calling his disciples friends instead of servants (or slaves in some translations), Jesus indicates an intimacy and equality not there in a servant-master relationship. It is, in fact, a new turn in their relationship to him. He is asking them to be like him. Later in this chapter he warns them that they will be hated, persecuted, put out of the synagogues and killed, all because of their love of him. He is asking of them their very lives.

* * *

What does it mean to lay down our lives for our friends? Like some other words of Jesus, this has become trite, trivialized, precisely because it is so foreign. We rarely experience such unselfish love. Yet history has provided many eamples of the power of willing sacrifice. Jesus, Jim Elliot, Martin Luther King, Jr., Oscar Romero—these persons have practiced unselfish, forgiving love as shown in their willingness to die for others.

Of course, it is unlikely that any of us will be called to personal martyrdom. But surely, the church is called to give up its life. And if we as communities of faith live up to Christ's calling, the church will often be hated, perhaps even persecuted by a world that doesn't understand that calling. Sadly enough, the church is sometimes inappropriately allied with the secular society and fails to witness to this sacrificial love. Whenever the church moves out of poor neighborhoods, opts to build bigger, more impressive buildings, decides to offer more recreation programs for its members, while refusing to address the violence and greed that permeate this culture, it is then that the church is denying rather than proclaiming the Christ.

Strangely, it is when the church is willing to lose its life for the sake of Christ that it bears real fruit.

As he struggled with what it meant to lay down his life for the Lord he loved, Archbishop Oscar Romero of El Salvador wrote:

> Those, who, in the Biblical phrase, would save their lives—that is, those who don't want commitments, who don't want to get into problems, who want to stay outside whatever demands our involvement—they will lose their lives." What a terrible thing to have lived well off, with no suffering, not getting into problems, quite tranquil, quite settled, with good connections—politically, economically, socially, lacking nothing, having everything. To what good? They will lose their lives. "But those who for love of me uproot themselves and accompany the people and go with the poor in their suffering and become incarnate and feel as their own the pain and the abuse—they will secure their lives because my Father will reward them. *(The Church Is All of You)*

It is so difficult for many people to see how they can be a part of the secular world and still maintain their citizenship in the Christian world. They fail to see Archbishop Romero's social justice ministry, the reason for his death, as a witness to Christ. But it is that.

Although Archbishop Romero was assasinated for his commitment to the Lord he loved and the people he served, the El Salvadoran people were strengthened and sustained by his witness, as were Christians all over Central America. "I appointed you to go on and bear fruit, fruit that shall last," says Jesus in John's Gospel. Wherever followers of Jesus are willing to lay down their lives for others, they are bearing the fruit that lasts.

Let us pray:
Loving God, who has given your Son's life for us, grant us the courage to love others with the kind of love that is willing to sacrifice. Help us bear fruit that will last, so that your Kingdom will come on earth. Amen.

June 4, 1995

READ IN YOUR BIBLE: Psalm 14
SUGGESTED PSALM: Same
SUGGESTED HYMNS: Holy God, We Praise Thy Name (E, F, L, P, UM, W)
  I Love Thy Kingdom, Lord (B, C, E, F, L, UM)

When Power Is Misused

The book of Psalms is essentially an anthology of religious poetry. The Hebrew title for the book is *Tehillim*, which means "Praises." One common theme is the celebration of the faithfulness, righteousness, greatness, and steadfast love of God. Another theme is supplication, whereby the people ask for God's help and healing. Psalm 14 is both a song of praise and a supplication. The psalm expresses faith in God's righteousness. God will be praised "when the LORD restores the fortunes of his people" (v. 7). Implicit in this psalm is a plea that things be set right soon.

Verses 1-3 express profound cynicism about the behavior of the whole human race. People don't really believe in God's justice; therefore, they break the commandments without qualm and collaborate in the corruption of the world. The harshest judgment is upon those who misuse power, "those evildoers who devour my people as if eating bread" (v. 4). The rest of the psalm looks forward to a time when God's justice will prevail.

It is important to note the essential human relationship with God. Verse 2 speaks of "seeking after God"; verse 3 about those who "do not call upon the Lord"; and verse 7 "when the Lord restores the fortunes of his people." Separation from God leads to evil throughout the land. But the Lord will honor those who remain with him.

* * *

It is easy to be cynical about people and nations—at least as easy now as it was in Old Testament times. A glance through the morning paper can convince us that "everyone is depraved, every deed is vile; no one does good!" (v. 1). Stories of theft, murder, greed, hatred, and vengeance make us shake our heads. We read of official lies masking illegal actions and of crimes committed by persons in positions of trust, and we wonder how God's beloved children can do so much harm.

Our tendancy is to identify the misuse of power with the rich, famous (or infamous) people in the headlines, and to forget that all of us have some power—perhaps more than we think. We have the power to hurt others, to withhold love, to abuse family members, to use money selfishly or hoard it greedily, to close our eyes to the suffering of others. We also have the power to pattern our lives after the example of Jesus. It is not only the "great" men and women of our day who abuse power. When we are foolish enough to act as if there were no God and no such thing as justice, we place ourselves in the company of the evildoers.

Several years ago I saw a play performed by a touring company of South African actors. It was called *Asinamali!* which means "We have no money!" This had been the rallying cry of the followers of a black African leader named Msizi Dube, who was gunned down before he could see the end of apartheid. "We have no money!" I have carried the phrase in my mind ever since; it is the voice of all the world's poor. When the psalmist says, "You would confound the plans of the poor, /but the LORD is their refuge" (v. 6), God speaks to me, not only to some evil dictator in a foreign country. Injustice is my business if there is anything I can do to alleviate it.

The cynic says there is nothing anyone can do. The world is evil and beyond salvation. But Psalm 14 calls us beyond cynicism to the confidence that "God is in the assembly of the righteous" (v. 5). There are those who remain in God's company and who seek to live in God's grace. For every wanderer in our modern world of sin and evil, there is a rescuer. For every evil deed, there is an act of loving kindness. The real question for us is Where am I? Do my thoughts and my actions place me in that assembly of the righteous, or in the company of the wicked and uncaring? Am I a wonderer or a rescuer?

Let us pray:
God of all people, forgive my foolishness. I sometimes forget that you do not exist to provide for my comfort and happiness. Help me to place myself on the side of justice, that I may become one of the righteous and not an evildoer. Amen.

June 11, 1995

READ IN YOUR BIBLE: Deuteronomy 6:5-15a
SUGGESTED PSALM: Psalm 92:1-10
SUGGESTED HYMNS: How Great Thou Art (B, F, L, P, UM)
   Holy, Holy, Holy! (all)

Whom Will You Follow?

The Old Testament is filled with laws, customs, rules, and commandments, some of which seem strange to modern readers. But in the sixth chapter of Deuteronomy all this is boiled down to a single, basic principle: we are to love God and to make the love of God the central fact of our lives. Jesus referred to these verses when he gave his own version of the essential law of life, adding "and your neighbor as yourself."

Moses had brought his people out of Egypt to a land that would be their home. After years in the wilderness and years before that in bondage to a foreign power, they needed guidance on how to live in harmony with God, each other, and the world. The book of Deuteronomy provided this by telling them exactly how to build their daily lives around a covenant relationship with God.

Many of the rules given in Deuteronomy reflect the conditions of life centuries before the birth of Christ. For example, the book comes out of a time when warfare meant hand-to-hand combat, and the existence of a tribal group might depend on success in battle with neighboring tribes. In Deuteronomy, the Israelites are commanded to conquer nearby towns and "not leave a soul alive" in them (20:16). Women were regarded as property in the ancient world, so it is assumed that they will have no say in the governing of the community and that they may become part of the spoils of war. In the economics of that time, still based largely on a barter system, it was forbidden to lend money at interest (23:19).

* * *

Rather than becoming lost in the details of the legal structure of that time and place, we need to consider the central message of this book, which is still relevant today. The choice to follow God and to live as God commands cannot be made once and for all. Every day, every minute, every choice we make is a choice for or against God.

It may be tempting for some Christians to read Deuteronomy and think that they could have an easier life if only there was such a rule book for modern living. Life is filled with so many choices. And decision making is so complicated. Even with a wonderful Bible we encounter frequent dilemmas.

Many Christians recall a time when they made a decision to accept Christ as their personal Savior. Such a moment is indeed significant, and can become a major turning point. Even this does not give us the cut-and-dried rules of conduct. It does not insolate us from having to make choices. Life goes on, and it is easy to wander off through the everyday details of our lives until we are far from the way we set out to follow. In each present moment, we choose to follow God's will or our own. Those who continually make right choices over a lifetime build a faith that can see them through anything.

During the riots in Los Angeles in the spring of 1992, Reginald Denny was pulled from the cab of his truck and beaten almost to death. Two men were eventually tried for attempted murder in this case. When Denny entered the courtroom to testify, his face was still visibly dented by the beating. He walked across that courtroom and stretched out a hand to the mother of one of the young men he had identified as his assailants. When she reached out in response, he suddenly hugged her. Both Denny and the mother of the accused had a choice in that moment, a choice between hatred and vindictiveness and a reconciling forgiveness. They chose to forgive.

Do we love God as we say we do? Real love grows slowly as we walk with the Beloved each day. Every choice we make, every thought and action either keeps us close to God or leads us away. Most of us will never have such a dramatic opportunity to follow Jesus as Reginald Denny did, we think. But the truth is that when we choose to follow Jesus or not, that is high drama.

Let us pray:
Lord of my life, grant that my love for you may grow strong through each moment, that I may someday know what it means to love you with all my heart, soul, and strength. Amen.

June 18, 1995

READ IN YOUR BIBLE: Micah 6:6-13
SUGGESTED PSALM: Psalm 52
SUGGESTED HYMNS: Be Thou My Vision (B, E, F, P, UM)
    Jesus Shall Reign (all)

Justice Corrupted

The prophet Micah had harsh words for those responsible for the injustices of his day, primarily those related to economics. He attacked those guilty of shady business practices, the liars, and those who attain wealth through violence. Addressing the people of a land threatened by Assyrian armies, Micah insisted that it was not so much the enemies from outside that Israel should fear, but its own corrupt citizens.

Jerusalem's busy marketplace was filled with goods from all over the ancient world: spices from Arabia, dried figs from Cyprus, cloth from Babylon, animals and slaves from many nations. Jewish merchants bought these goods for resale to their own people and traveling traders. It must have been easy enough to cheat a little on weights and measures, or to lie about the quality of items for sale. Armed robbery was not uncommon on the lonely roads leading into the city.

If Jerusalem's prosperity was based on such practices, then all its citizens except the very poor were implicated in its crimes. The dissension and enmity inevitable in such an atmosphere would make it hard for the city to resist an attack, and eventually Jerusalem was bound to be conquered. The invaders could even be seen as instruments of God's justice.

* * *

"Justice, sir, is the great interest of man on earth," said the famous American statesman Daniel Webster *(On Mr. Justice Story,* September 12, 1845). All of us want to be treated justly; no one enjoys feeling like a victim of gross injustice. The problem comes in deciding what is just and in arriving at a way to provide equal justice to all.

We tend to think of justice as an abstraction, something hard to define and even harder to achieve. Micah speaks of justice not as something only to think about or believe in, but as something to *do*. Action is the requirement: "[The Lord] has told you O mortal what is good; /and what does the LORD require of you /but to do justice" (v. 8).

Like the prosperous merchants of Micah's day, we try to make our peace with God through pious words, elaborate acts of worship, or the kind of charity that reflects a guilty conscience. All that is meaningless unless we learn to "act justly."

What does it mean to act justly? This is very difficult to determine if we begin by believing that we should have priority in determing justice. If we must have our claims settled first; if we must be satisfied first; if we must receive the first share, justice will be a long time coming. Justice happens when we make the welfare of others a priority for us.

What does it look like to act justly? A small-town lawyer discovers that in his community there is no provision for legal representation of those who cannot afford to pay a lawyer. Recognizing that the legal system cannot work unless all are able to participate equally, he approaches fellow lawyers in the area and sets up a rotation for representing those who need to go to court but are unable to pay. A retired contractor donates time and skills to Habitat for Humanity, helping those who need affordable housing to reach their goal. A grandmother helps raise money for a shelter for victims of domestic violence. A teenager finds a wallet on the street and returns it, intact, to its rightful owner.

Micah tells us that justice is not an abstraction. Justice—and injustice—are all around us, part of our everyday experience. We must train ourselves to inspect our everyday activity through a "justicescope." Will anyone be hurt by my action? Will anyone be hurt by my inaction? Injustice carries within it the means of its own correction. That means is usually painful and sometimes fatal. We mortals know what God requires of us; we would be wise to follow the instruction in the book of Micah before it is too late for our own cities and nations.

Let us pray:
O God, we know that you are just as well as merciful. Show us how to act justly, as individuals and as citizens of our communities, that our lives may reflect your will. Amen.

June 25, 1995

READ IN YOUR BIBLE: 1 Thessalonians 5:8-18
SUGGESTED PSALM: Psalm 65
SUGGESTED HYMNS: The King of Love My Shepherd Is (E, L, P, UM, W)
It Came Upon the Midnight Clear (all)

Sharing the Good News

When Paul and his helpers set out to take the good news of the gospel throughout the world, the task must have seemed impossible. They were mocked, threatened, attacked, jailed, and many of them were executed. The converts they did make faced the same perils.

In his first letter to the Thessalonians, Paul reminds the little group of Christians in that Greek seaport what the good news is: "God has not destined us for wrath, but for obtaining salvation through our Lord Jesus Christ who died for us so that whether we are awake or asleep we may live with him" (vv. 9-10).

Paul then urges the Thessalonians to support and encourage each other, so that the church may be a place of refreshment and a source of strength. Always the practical person, Paul ackowledges that there will be difficult times and persons who will be lazy, fainthearted, and weak. He urges patience and peace among them. In order to evangelize a hostile city, they will need each other.

Paul reminds the followers to find help in constant prayer. And he encourages them to remain a people of rejoicing no matter what the circumstance. Prayer, peace, patience, encouragement, joy. Paul has tried to provide everything necessary for survival of the community.

* * *

Bad news travels fast. When a natural disaster strikes, or a hideous accident occurs, or an armed conflict breaks out, the news seems to spread effortlessly and with lightning speed. Somehow, we are not so eager to spread good news. People seem less interested, less inclined to believe it. Those who have already benefited from the good news may want to keep it to themselves.

Paul's instructions, if followed, would raise the spirit and strengthen the mission of most modern churches. Too often today, as in Paul's time, the church becomes a center of dissension instead of a loving community of faith. Lay and clergy leaders are attacked rather than supported. Disgruntled members hold secret meetings, resign noisily, or even start splinter groups to compete with the original body.

Yet the good news of salvation through Jesus Christ must be shared. We may want to keep it to ourselves, or to people like us, or to those who believe and behave exactly as we do, but the gospel will not be confined in any narrow creed. When we try to imprison it, we turn the good news into bad news.

In the spring and summer of 1993, the Midwestern United States was devastated by floods. Inevitably, various religious leaders claimed that the floods were God's punishment for whatever sins that group was most eager to condemn. These judges conveniently ignored the fact that thousands of persons not involved in their "pet" sins were also harmed by the floods. These preachers of bad news seemed to have forgotten Paul's words: "God has not destined us for wrath" (v. 9).

The unexplainable bad news in our lives seems to draw us into finding blame. Bad actions always lead to bad consequences. And these bad consequences are always God's punishment.

On the contrary, the good news is that God intends a full, productive, and meaningful life for every person in this world and an eternity of joy and peace when this life ends. To be sure, those who reject God's loving guidance will suffer the consequences, but it is not for the church or its members to pass judgment. We can safely leave that to God. Our mission is to share the good news.

Paul tells the Thessalonians to "give thanks whatever happens" (v. 18) because it is God's will that we appreciate the gift of life with all its joys and sorrows. Only with that attitude of gratitude can we become worthy to spread the news with which God has entrusted us.

Let us pray:

Loving God, thank you for the good news given to me and to all creation in Christ Jesus. Teach me how to share this news with others. Make me one of those who encourages and supports; help me to give thanks whatever happens. Amen.

July 2, 1995

READ IN YOUR BIBLE: Psalm 82
SUGGESTED PSALM: Same
SUGGESTED HYMNS: God of the Ages (B, E, F, L, P, UM, W)
America the Beautiful (B, C, E, F, P, UM, W)

Condemnation for National Wrongs

Judaism began in a polytheistic world; the early Hebrews believed in the existence of other gods. YHWH was their national god. Other nations had their own gods.

Psalm 82 begins with the God of Israel sitting in a court with all the other gods and raising questions of justice. YHWH accuses these other gods of allowing the wicked to triumph on earth while the weak have no one to act on their behalf. This Jewish God has a moral dimension lacking in all the others. Indeed, most of the gods of the ancient world were simply human beings with supernatural powers. They had temper tantrums, fell in love with mortals, went to war with each other, and achieved their goals through deceit and betrayal.

"They have neither knowledge nor understanding, /they walk around in darkness; /all the foundations of the earth are shaken," says the God of the Hebrews. "You are gods /children of the Most High, all of you; /nevertheless, you shall die like mortals, /and fall like any prince" (vv. 5-7). In that moment YHWH the tribal god becomes God, the Lord of the universe. The psalmist invites God to judge the whole earth—not just the tribes of Israel, "for all the nations are yours" (v. 8).

* * *

It is in this ethical dimension that the God of the Old Testament comes to us today, still demanding justice for the victims of oppression and evil. God reminds us that nations built on injustice cannot stand forever, any more than individuals can build fulfilling lives on morally bankrupt values. Although tyranny may seem to win for a time, in the end God's justice will prevail.

Recently I toured Berlin and saw the Reichstag, once a symbol of Nazi power, now a seat of government in a free Germany. I also visited Checkpoint Charlie, for many years the main passage between East and West Germany. There is still a remnant of the Wall there as a reminder of the past. Nearby is a small museum displaying among other things the ingenious methods by which a few East Germans managed to escape to the West. Cars are shown with secret compartments built to conceal escapees. There are photographs of a hot air balloon in which one family managed to sail over the wall. Perhaps the most unusual display is a pair of suitcases built to be carried together with a person inside, her torso and head in the front suitcase and her legs in the back.

All of these escape strategies foreshadowed the outcome of an enslaving government. Its power was never total. It was continually weakened until it collapsed. Unjust societies always fail because people will not submit forever. Victims eventually demand justice, and with God's help justice is finally done.

As we celebrate the founding of our great country, we are rightly proud of two centuries of striving for justice. Our nation was born for this very reason. And we have continued to examine ourselves and seek justice; freedom for our own people, universal social security, economic resources around the world, and democracy for people in other lands.

But we should not be self-righteous as we watch the disintegration of the former communist bloc. We continue to have our own forms of injustice. As long as there is hunger, racism, unequal access to the courts, and unattainable health care, our society has not attained complete justice. Although the walls that divide us may not be as obvious as the one that separated East and West Berlin, they are every bit as effective.

The psalmist reminds us that the God of the Jews became the God of the whole world because this God upholds righteousness and condemns wickedness. If we say we worship God, we must also work to bring justice to our communities and our nations. "Rise up, O God, judge the earth; for all the nations belong to you!" (v. 8).

Let us pray:
God of the universe, we pray for justice throughout your world. Show us how we can make a difference, that your will may be done on earth as it is in heaven. Amen.

July 9, 1995

READ IN YOUR BIBLE: Amos 5:6–15
SUGGESTED PSALM: Psalm 63
SUGGESTED HYMNS: Open My Eyes, That I May See (B, C, F, P, UM)
God, Who Stretched the Spangled Heavens (B, E, L, P, UM, W)

Working for Justice and Righteousness

The God of Amos is not the friend who strolls with us in the garden or pets woolly lambs. This is a God of power whose patience has run out. God is a Creator whose world contains a moral order as well as a natural order. As night follows day, punishment follows wrongdoing; as fire and flood spread, destruction will spread over those who break God's laws.

The laws that concerned Amos dealt with the abuse of power and wealth. God's wrath was directed specifically at "you that turn justice to poison and thrust righteousness to the ground" (v. 7). Amos looked at the Jewish society of his day and saw a growing gap between rich and poor, manipulation of the court system by the wealthy to the disadvantage of the destitute, and a general lack of concern for justice. He also saw enemy armies advancing on his little country and recognized that "it is an evil time" (v. 13). The only hope was for Israel's mighty God to come to their aid—but why would God do that, when the people in power were flouting God's laws and ignoring the warnings of the prophets?

The command of God is clearly stated more than once in this passage: "Make your way to the LORD" (v. 6); "seek good and not evil" (v. 14); "hate evil, and love good; establish justice in the courts" (v. 15). However, no one seemed to be listening.

* * *

If God works through human history as Amos believed, every event has consequences for good or evil, and those consequences extend for a very long time. The challenge for the Christian is to try to determine what justice means in this time and place, and then work diligently to achieve it.

Look at the headlines in today's newspaper. They will quickly suggest some issues that involve justice and injustice. Then ask two questions. What does God say to our society, to the church, to me about this issue? What can I do to act in accordance with God's will for justice?

One simple thing anyone can do is to pray while reading the newspaper. When a particular story touches you, stop and say a prayer for the people involved. When you are puzzled about the right and wrong of a situation, ask God to help you understand. When you see a clear case of injustice, open yourself to guidance about what you might do to help correct it.

A former governor of my state became convinced that the Native American population had been treated unjustly for many years, and that something must be done to change the situation. Soon after becoming governor, George Mickelson declared a "Year of Reconciliation" between Native Americans and others in our state. A commission was established, made up of representatives of both groups, and it began working to create a more just society for all. When Governor Mickelson was killed in a plane crash in 1992, those who had been involved in these efforts resolved to carry on in his memory. His life made a difference in this state because of his convictions.

Who hasn't heard of Mother Teresa of Calcutta? A fragile young woman from Yugoslavia served her God quietly in a religious order. God opened her eyes and her heart to the poorest of the poor in India. She responded to God's call, and even had to fight the religious hierarchy to get permission to serve. You know the rest of her remarkable servanthood.

Most of us do not have the opportunity to lead a state or a nation. Nor will we minister so spectacularly that the whole world will know us, but we, too, can make a difference if we become resolved to work for justice and righteousness. Floods, fires, earthquakes all bring out the Red Cross and church disaster services. Sometimes hundreds, and even thousands, of people without excuses for inaction provide food, shelter, clothing, medicine, and labor. That is ministry. And there are countless other ways you and others can and do serve daily. God notices.

Let us pray:
Help me, Lord, to seek good and not evil, that I may live and do my part to work for justice in your world. Amen.

July 16, 1995

READ IN YOUR BIBLE: Romans 5:1-11
SUGGESTED PSALM: Psalm 123
SUGGESTED HYMNS: There's a Wideness in God's Mercy (all)
Savior, Like a Shepherd Lead Us (B, C, E, F, L, P, UM)

Demonstrating Undeserved Love

Broken relationships can be restored through love and forgiveness; indeed, that is the only way they can be restored. Paul tells us that this truth applies not only to our human relationships, but also to our relationship with God.

The book of Romans was addressed to a little group of Christians who were somehow holding fast to their faith even though most people in their community not only did not share this faith but disapproved of it. In fact, membership in the Christian community placed the security, the property, and even the lives of these people in danger. What could give them the courage to persevere in spite of this?

Paul saw that he could encourage the Romans by reminding them of Jesus, "through whom we obtained access to this grace in which we stand" (v. 2). He dared to suggest that by grace God could turn their very suffering into a blessing, since "suffering produces endurance, and endurance produces character, and character produces hope" (v. 3-4). In other words, with God's help we can be made stronger and more worthy by the painful and frightening experiences of our lives. Note that there is no promise to exempt the followers of Jesus from suffering. What is promised is a way to make suffering meaningful.

* * *

Some people are born with a nervous system that does not pass sensation from their skin to their brain. They feel no pain. At first this sounds wonderful. But very quickly this turns into a nightmare. Faulty nerves fail to tell a baby that formula is too hot and is burning as it is swallowed. Faulty nerves do not tell a toddler who has fallen that he is bleeding from the back of his head. Faulty nerves fail to tell an older adult that a stress fracture needs immediate attention. Pain has its place in life.

Most of us would like to avoid pain. We certainly don't go looking for it. Yet inevitably life deals its blows, and at times we wonder what possible benefit to us or to others can be derived from tragedy. The book of Romans tells us that there are lessons we can only learn through suffering: lessons of grace and forgiveness and undeserved love.

Much of our pain results from the fact that we live in an imperfect world and are born into a sinful community. Since the days of Adam and Eve, human beings have more or less botched the mission God gave us when we were created. Sin is part of our inheritance—but so is love, so is grace, so is the chance to do better and to find our way back to God. As Jesus transformed the cross from an instrument of torture into a symbol of salvation, so we can transform the trials of our lives.

A television program featured interviews with children of Nazi leaders. Now mature adults, they had been youngsters during World War II. Most of them said they'd had no idea of the crimes being committed by their parents—yet they were wracked with guilt when they recalled the horrors perpetrated by men they had known as kindly elders.

Each one in his or her own way seemed to try to find a way to bring good out of the evil of the past. A nephew of Heinrich Heidrich has devoted his life to presenting the works of artists who were killed by his uncle. The son of Martin Boorman became a Catholic priest. Asked whether they could forgive the men who had done such terrible things and whose memory blighted their own lives, the group was silent for a moment. Then Boorman said, "It is absolutely necessary to forgive."

God continues to love and bless us, though we don't deserve it. Knowing this, we must learn to forgive and love those who hurt us as well, to work for reconciliation among all God's people. We can probably never love (in the sense of warmth and affection) those who commit hideous crimes. But if we truly love God we can respond to God's undeserved love for all creation. Is there someone just waiting for your forgiveness? For what do you wish to be forgiven?

Let us pray:
Loving God, teach me to love as you do, not holding grudges or demanding reciprocity, but completely freely, giving as I have received from you. Amen.

July 23, 1995

READ IN YOUR BIBLE: Psalm 103:6–14
SUGGESTED PSALM: Same
SUGGESTED HYMNS: Dear Lord and Father of Mankind (B, C, E, F, L, P, UM)
Praise, My Soul, the King of Heaven (B, E, F, L, P, UM, W)

Experiencing Undeserved Love

Religions of the world have always struggled with one basic question: What is God like? Well, our God wants us to know who he is. "He made known his ways to Moses" (v. 6). In a series of adjectives, the psalmist answers that question for the Judaic tradition: God is just, mighty, gracious, slow to anger, steadfastly loving, and compassionate.

Parts of the Old Testament emphasize the first two of these adjectives, stressing God's power and demand for obedience. In Psalm 103, they come first in the list of God's aspects. Some passages of the Old Testament and most of the New Testament, while holding to these qualities as important aspects of God's nature, place more significance on the final part of the description. In this Psalm, the order of the aspects is overwhelmed by the number of allusions to God's kinder qualities. The psalmist repeats the basic idea of God's compassion later in Psalm 103: "As a father has compassion for his children, / so the LORD has compassion for his children" (v. 13).

The Latin root of the word *passion* means "to suffer," while the prefix *com* means "with." Thus to have compassion means to suffer with someone else, to feel the pain of another.

* * *

Anyone who has been a parent knows the lengths to which parental love will go, the difficulty of balancing healthy discipline with the desire to give love and support. Parents know the ache of love for an undeserving child, the stab of disappointment when a child does not live up to fond expectations. Parents know what it is to "suffer with" a troubled son or daughter. They seem to absorb all of the child's difficulty, but that absorption doesn't remove the child's pain, as they wish it would.

Psalm 103 tells us that God feels that way about every human being, every one of us "prodigal" children. God suffers and grieves over our trials and does everything possible to "make it all better."

People respond differently to this kind of undeserved love. Some can't believe in it, and go on trying somehow to earn the love they need. Some may resent an in-spite-of-everything love that implies they are not perfect. Others are merely grateful. For those who can accept it, the love of parents and of God becomes a kind of spiritual home, a precious sense of wellbeing that one can always return to in time of need.

Robert Frost, in his poem "The Death of the Hired Man," offers two definitions of *home*. One is this: "Home is where when you have to go there, they have to take you in." This suggests a love based on duty, a sort of gritting of the teeth as love is offered, a love that says "You aren't worthy, but you're mine, so I'll help you out." Recipients of this kind of love will probably resent it and feel trapped by it.

Frost's other definition of home is "something you haven't to deserve." This comes much closer to the biblical picture of a heavenly parent. As Psalm 103 puts it, "he will not always accuse /nor will he keep his anger forever" (v. 9). God does not hold grudges as we too often do. God does not go on holding our sins against us. In fact, our sins are irrelevant to the love God showers upon us. In the home God keeps for us, love is "something you haven't to deserve."

This is true because God suffers with us, "he knows how we were made, he remembers that we are but dust" (v. 14). The ultimate expression of this kind of love was given when Jesus prayed for his executioners: "Forgive them; for they do not know what they are doing" (Luke 23:34). We don't have to deserve God's love; we only need to let it transform us.

Complete transformation is more than accepting the gift of unmerited love. It means giving it as well. We need to transform the familiar expression "guilty by association" into "forgiven and loved by association." If God forgives and loves each of us, then God's choice to do so should be enough to motivate us to do so as well.

Let us pray:
Thank you, heavenly Father, for loving me in spite of my unworthiness. Help me to love others even when I think they don't deserve it. Amen.

July 30, 1995

READ IN YOUR BIBLE: Micah 2:1–7
SUGGESTED PSALM: Psalm 49
SUGGESTED HYMNS: God of Grace and God of Glory (B, C, E, F, L, P, UM)
What Wondrous Love Is This (B, E, F, L, P, UM, W)

Beware of Greed

Micah paints a sinister picture of corrupt people lying awake at night planning ways to steal the property of others, then getting up at dawn to put those plans into action. But God is willing to fashion a plot against such wickedness. God will punish such people, says the prophet. God's judgment will fall on the whole nation of Israel, because it not only allows these injustices to exist but actually encourages them by overvaluing money and property.

Micah questions the people: "Is the LORD's patience exhausted?" (v. 7). He did not speak only to the leaders, for the leaders would be nothing without their followers. Micah's warning was for everyone: "Thus says the LORD: /Now, I am devising against this family, an evil /from which you cannot remove your necks" (v. 3).

Micah saw that his nation was moving in the wrong direction. The people did not believe that God would punish their avarice. Micah counseled them not to believe that "disgrace will not overtake us" (v. 6). Not only did they reject the notion that they were guilty, but they also rejected any idea that they could be punished.

* * *

Is it fair for many to suffer for the sins of a few? Fair or not, the consequences of evil acts sometimes do affect the innocent as well as the guilty. All taxpayers in the U.S. have had to pay more taxes as a result of the Savings and Loan crisis, which was caused by the greed of a few. When the environment is injured by the dumping of toxic waste, all of us risk our health, and all must help pay to clean up the site. In many ways, the sins of a few cause harm to all.

Like the Israelites in Micah's day, many people have become obsessed with acquiring material possessions. We desire more than the necessities of life, which most of us can earn through our labor. We want the latest technologies, the biggest houses, the most elaborate tools, the most sylish clothing, the most powerful automobiles. When we can't get what we want through a paycheck, we look for ways to cheat on our taxes, or we dream of winning a fortune through one of the gambling schemes that have become so popular. If I haven't named your vice, seriously think now about your own personal expression of greed.

Recently newspapers carried the story of a Pennsylvania man who won more than sixteen million dollars in a state lottery. A few years later he was broke, with creditors threatening to take his house away. Even worse, his brother had been arrested for trying to hire someone to kill him, so that the brother might inherit future prize payments.

Greed does terrible things to people and to nations. It creates desires that cannot be satisfied because the desires increase faster than the means to fulfill them. D. H. Lawrence once wrote a story called "The Rocking Horse Winner" in which a small boy imagines that the walls of his home whisper, "There must be more money." Many children today grow up in homes that seem to whisper the same words, and not all of them live in conditions of poverty.

A Spanish proverb says, "A dog with money is addressed as Mr. Dog." What we want with money is not so much the things it will buy but the status we think we will gain by having things. Greed is destructive because it puts false values at the very center of our lives. It makes us believe that we can buy self-respect and the regard of others. It encourages us to imagine that the wealthy deserve their wealth and the poor are poor because they are less deserving. It deludes us into worshiping the golden calf instead of God. Jesus put it bluntly: "You cannot serve God and wealth" (Matthew 6:24).

What is really of value is a sense of self-esteem, which does not come from the accumulation of things. We need a self-esteem that promotes us no matter what we possess.

Let us pray:
Giver of life, help me to let go of the false values that make me want more than my share of the world's goods. Teach me to replace my greed with generosity. Amen.

August 6, 1995

READ IN YOUR BIBLE: Isaiah 55:6–11
SUGGESTED PSALM: Psalm 103
SUGGESTED HYMNS: Praise, My Soul, the King of Heaven (B, E, F, L, P, UM, W)
O Worship the King (B, C, E, F, L, P, UM)

Responding to God's Call

The book of Isaiah was compiled after the Hebrew people had returned from exile in Babylon. Isaiah believed that the events of the time had to be seen in the context of God's plan for the redemption of all people. This book takes us far beyond the tribal God of earlier writings to a universal deity.

The Hebrews had struggled to understand why God would allow them to be conquered and taken prisoner to a strange land. The message of the prophets was that their own disobedience to God's laws had caused these events. Isaiah adds another dimension to this message. He presents a vision of resurrection after suffering, a hope for salvation and rebirth that was fully realized in the life, death, and resurrection of Jesus.

Isaiah tells us to "seek the LORD while he may be found, /call upon him while he is near" (v. 6). But if God is present, why the search? Isaiah explains the problem in terms of the vast difference between the creator of the universe and a human being: "For my thoughts are not your thoughts, /nor are your ways my ways" (v. 8).

* * *

The problem of searching for God is not a question of his absence but our limited understanding of God. When we cannot "find God," we are usually trying to find an overgrown human being we have created in our own minds, a sort of genie in a bottle whose power we can control and use.

Sometimes people spend their lives wandering from church to church, from creed to creed, from leader to leader, seeking God. Others conclude early in life that the search is useless, because there is no God. Still others seek God only in times of crisis and are disappointed when they do not get what they want: specific, predetermined responses to their prayers. A few even seek God in a physical way. One of the Russian cosmonauts commented after his first trip into space that he had looked around up there but had not seen God.

This passage from Isaiah is not so much an explanation of how to call for God as it is a statement of faith that God is calling us. "Let the wicked forsake their way, /and the unrighteous their thoughts; /let them return to the LORD, /that he may have mercy on them" (v. 7). God calls us to do the things we already know are right. God is not lost; we are.

A small boy asked his mother, "Is God everywhere?" "Yes," she answered. "Is God in the floor?" "I suppose so," she said. "If God is in the floor," the boy asked, "can I walk on him with my muddy boots?"

We quickly see this small child's error. He was confusing God's being everywhere with God's being everything. God was there, but God wasn't the floor. Adults make a similar error when we say about the tragic death of a child, "God must have needed her in heaven." God may have been present at her death and may have been ready to receive her, but that does not mean that God willed the suffering and death of a child.

We may smile at the child's question, but our own understanding of God often seems as unsophisticated. We tinker with prayer formulas, trying to get the words right so God will satisfy our desires. We argue about God's gender or language, as if these human attributes could limit the Maker of heaven and earth. "But as the heavens are high above the earth, so are my ways high above your ways" (v. 9).

God has made available as much understanding as we need to live satisfying, productive lives. The scriptures, the teachings of the church, and our own reason and experience tell us how we should use the days that have been given to us. There is still so much that we don't know, but to believe that we could ever know everything is foolish. It is wanting to be God. God calls us to make a journey toward him, to move on in *faith* not *knowledge*. We are assured that God's purposes will be accomplished.

Let us pray:
Lord of all that is, save me from trying to make you over into a God I can understand fully. Open me to your call today and every day, that I may follow the way you have shown. Amen.

August 13, 1995
READ IN YOUR BIBLE: Psalm 125:1–5
SUGGESTED PSALM: Same
SUGGESTED HYMNS: Beneath the Cross of Jesus (all)
                      Eternal Father, Strong to Save (B, E, F, L, P)

Only God Can Protect

Psalm 125 comes from a time when Israel was threatened by many foreign enemies. The people were fearful, and with good reason. Israel was surrounded by enemies, all of them bigger and more powerful. This psalm directly addresses being surrounded. But it turns the fear of the enemy into the reassurance of being surrounded by protective mountains. The message is that if they put their trust in God, all will be well. The challenge is for them to develop an inner strength based on faith, so that no matter what happens, they will be able to rely on God to protect them. "Those who trust in the LORD are like Mount Zion," says the psalmist, "which cannot be moved, but abides forever" (v. 1).

The psalmist reminds the people of God's promise that they will inherit and occupy the land (v. 3). It belongs to the righteous as long as they remain obedient.

This kind of faith is based on integrity. The person of genuine faith does not say one thing and do another, but is "upright in their hearts" (v. 4). Such people do the right thing because it is right, not because it is easy or pleasant. God is with them because they are with God.

* * *

The psalm does not promise that we will have no problems or that good people will always have easy, comfortable lives. It says that the mountain cannot be moved. It does not say that there will never be fierce storms. A friend I admired for her steadfastness told me that in dark days she would ask herself, "Who are you to be immune to the troubles of this world?" We don't need faith when the sun is shining and our side is winning.

It is natural to pray that God will "do good . . . to the good" (v. 4) and punish the wicked. It's also natural for us to assume that we are among the good and that the wicked are those other people, the ones who don't behave as we do or who look different or think in different ways. If we saw ourselves as evildoers, we would probably pray for mercy rather than justice.

Some people become cynical and fearful as the years pass. Having been unable to cope with the losses they have suffered, they clutch their remaining treasures protectively. Having been forced by circumstances to experience unwelcome change, they view all change as a threat. Such persons may have defined faith in a magical way, as a means of getting God to make them happy. When faith does not seem to "work" in this way, it is lost as easily as a belief in Santa Claus or reliance on a lucky charm.

Other people's faith grows stronger as they grow older. Experience has taught them that with God's help they can weather all life's storms, even turn the worst difficulties into opportunities for deeper communion with God. Like athletes, they understand the truth of the saying "no pain, no gain." They welcome each stage of life as a new adventure in faith.

Alfred, Lord Tennyson, wrote a poem about the Greek hero Ulysses in old age. He imagined Ulysses as a sort of retired king, hanging around the palace with nothing much to do, watching his son Telemachus make all the real decisions. Finally, Tennyson has Ulysses gather up the old sailors who had served with him, fit out a new ship, and make ready to launch it into unknown waters. The poem ends with Ulysses' speech to his men:

> Though much is taken, much abides; and though
> We are not now that strength which in old days
> Moved earth and heaven, that which we are, we are.

The Christian remembers who he or she is: God's beloved child. And "though much is taken" as years pass, "much abides." The last words spoken by John Wesley, founder of the Methodist movement, were "Best of all is, God is with us." Such a faith can see us through anything.

Let us pray:
God of all the seasons of my life, help me to grow in the simple trust that you are with me always, and that your love will always sustain me. Amen.

August 20, 1995

READ IN YOUR BIBLE: Psalm 2
SUGGESTED PSALM: Same
SUGGESTED HYMNS: Jesus Calls Us O'er the Tumult (B, C, E, F, L, UM)
The God of Abraham Praise (B, E, L, P, UM, W)

Fair Warning

Psalm 2 gives a disturbing picture of God laughing at human affairs: "He who sits in the heavens laughs; /the LORD has them in derision" (v. 4). *Them* refers to leaders who created the tangle of national alliances and enmities, wars and treaties that was the ancient world. After the laughter comes anger at the unrighteous and reassurances for God's people. Conspiracies will fail eventually, and those who use armies to oppress the weak are doomed. God is moving through the events of history.

The ancient Jews, a small nation surrounded by larger, better armed countries, must have felt terribly vulnerable. Only with God's help could they hope to survive. No doubt Psalm 2 was meant to encourage them in dangerous times: "Happy are all who take refuge in him" (v. 12)!

The dream of peace is as old as the reality of war. However, we usually imagine a peace secured by victory—the victory of our side. So the Hebrews looked forward to the day when God would say to them: "I will make the nations your heritage, /and the ends of the earth your possession. /You shall break them with a rod of iron, /and dash them in pieces like a potter's vessel" (vv. 8-9). Peace would come after success in war.

* * *

The Middle East has been the scene of struggle for thousands of years. The recent war in the Persian Gulf took place in some of the same areas where biblical wars were fought. It is hard to remember a time when there was no armed conflict in this region, which has always been contested by competing peoples and religious groups. With modern telecommunications and jet travel, disputes in the Holy Land are no longer distant and no longer the concern of only the local Israelis and Arabs.

Peace following war is a common idea today. When the great

powers of the communist world began to crumble, it seemed as though there was finally a chance for an end to the world's divisions. The West had won the cold war. Now the whole family of nations could work together to create a new era of peace and justice. Why not?

We quickly learned that all the underlying problems remained. Those things that separate us into classes, that point to our differences rather than our similarities continue to breed conflict that escalates into war. Poverty, ethnic and religious bigotry, racial hatred, violence, greed, and materialism did not end with the end of communism.

The communist ideology had tried to eliminate these problems, and it had not been entirely unsuccessful. Friends from East Germany have told me that in some ways life was better before the wall came down. Everyone had food, shelter, and work. Public transportation, health care, and child care were available to all. While they would not like to see a return to the political oppression they lived with before, they seem unsure whether the sudden change to capitalism will be totally beneficial.

The psalmist reminds us that any real progress must be based on faith and obedience. "O Kings, be wise," he says, "be warned, O rulers of the earth. /Serve the LORD with fear" (vv. 10-11).

Who can dispute that we have had fair warning to mend our ways? The Bible is filled with the word of repentence. Our history books are filled with the tales of people and nations who did not obey and suffered bad consequences. And our personal life stories make a catalog of offenses and results.

Frontier churches used to have a bench called the "anxious seat," reserved for worshipers who had been affected by the preaching and who were concerned enough to repent. We might well examine the turmoil of our world from the anxious seat. From there we might see more clearly our need to repent. God has given us fair warning.

Let us pray:
God of history, help us to learn the lessons of the past so that we can help to build a better future. Give us a vision of a just society and show us how to do our part to create it. Amen.

August 27, 1995
READ IN YOUR BIBLE: Deuteronomy 8:11-20
SUGGESTED PSALM: Psalm 106:19-31
SUGGESTED HYMNS: O Worship the King (B, C, E, F, L, P, UM)
Holy God, We Praise Thy Name (E, F, L, P, UM, W)

Disobedience Brings Destruction

The Jews had been through much as a people by the time Moses brought them to the edge of the promised land. Now they were on the brink of realizing all their hopes. How easy it would be to say, "This is the mark of God's favor, God's reward to us for our courage and perseverance." Instead, Moses instructed them to "Remember the LORD your God, for it is he who gives you power to get wealth" (v. 18).

The good life could even result in their worshiping other gods. Moses told them further: "If you do forget the LORD your God and follow other gods to serve and worship them, I solemnly warn you today that you shall surely perish" (v. 19). Sure enough, once settled in the promised land the Hebrew people began to worship the idols of their enemies. Why take the chance of losing all they had gained? It couldn't hurt to worship Baal and other gods as well as the Lord. But this new worship led them to behave as the Canaanites did, to take on the values of their neighbors and forget the laws God had given them. Eventually, the nation created by Moses and his successors was destroyed.

* * *

The chief danger of prosperity is in forgetting how it came to us. No one gains wealth totally through hard work and personal merit. The wealthy person has been helped along the way by inheritance, someone else's kindness, or sheer luck; or that person has achieved success at the expense of others who have been exploited. Christians also believe that God aids us in building productive lives. We need to remember who we are and not be deluded into the thinking that we deserve to be better off than others.

Modern people are as susceptible to the temptation to worship other gods as the ancient Hebrews were. We may not call them gods. They may not look like the ancient gods with their human or animal "personalities." But they function just as the gods of old. We are enticed and coerced as we worship at the altar of money or power or narrow patriotism or personal security or family loyalty or some human leader. When we bow down and worship something that is not God, we worship idols.

Every year or so the students in American schools are asked to list their heroes, the persons they look to as role models. The results can be disturbing; usually, the winners of the poll are the stars of sports, the media, and popular music. Great writers, educators, scientists, and ethicists are conspicuously absent from the list. We have become a society that worships celebrity rather than integrity. The "stars" of our culture are those who achieve wealth and status, not necessarily those who contribute to the betterment of the world.

Adults are not immune to this tendancy. Too often we follow the political leaders who tell us what we want to hear, those who pander to our love of comfort and success, even when we never believed their promises or when we know that short-term gains only postpone disaster.

So where is the destruction forecast for those who follow false gods? It is all about us. Destruction is in the schools, where self-gratification is worshiped and where respect for teachers and administrators is only a memory of the past. Destruction is on the streets, where cocaine is the name of a modern god. Destruction is in the homes of everyone who builds an altar to the credit card. Destruction is in churches where pastors replace God instead of lead others to him.

Who will you follow? The nations of the earth are as mortal as we are; power and wealth pass eventually into other hands; nature erodes the things we build. The only eternal kingdom is God's, and that must exist in our hearts.

Our hope is in remembering God through the good times so that God will remember and help us when we once again need a strength that is greater than our own.

Let us pray:
God of both prosperity and want, keep me close to you no matter what befalls me. Restrain me when I am tempted to worship other gods, for you alone are holy and eternal. Amen.

Contributors

March–May
Joan Laney is very actively involved in Good Samaritan United Methodist Church in Memphis, Tennessee, a recently chartered interracial congregation. Joan formerly taught writing at The University of Evansville and Indiana University of Evansville, and the University of Illinois. She is a contributing author to *365 Meditations for Mothers of Young Children*, published by Dimensions for Living.

September–November
David Mosser is pastor of University United Methodist Church in Georgetown, Texas. He is a frequent instructor in Women's Schools of Christian Mission. A contributor to *The International Lesson Annual, 1994–95*, he has also published enrichment articles, homiletical helps, and Bible studies in a variety of pastoral journals, including *Quarterly Review*.

December–February
Jeffrey A. Rasche is pastor of San Jose United Methodist Church in San Jose, Illinois. He has written extensively for the *United Methodist Reporter* and The United Methodist Publishing House. His work includes *Jr. High Trek, Directions in Faith, Teacher in the Church Today, Youth Magazine,* and Bible lessons and daily meditations for *Mature Years* magazine. He has also written over 200 articles for a variety of secular magazines and newspapers.

June–August

Nancy Veglahn is currently a full professor of English at South Dakota State University in Brookings, South Dakota, teaching courses in writing, literature, and children's literature. She is the author of fourteen juvenile books and a winner of the New York *Herald-Tribune* "Honor Book" award. She has also written Bible lessons and daily meditations for *Mature Years* magazine.